Contents

S0-BQY-650

Don't be a Hamster!

30 Ways to Spark the Imagination of Busy People

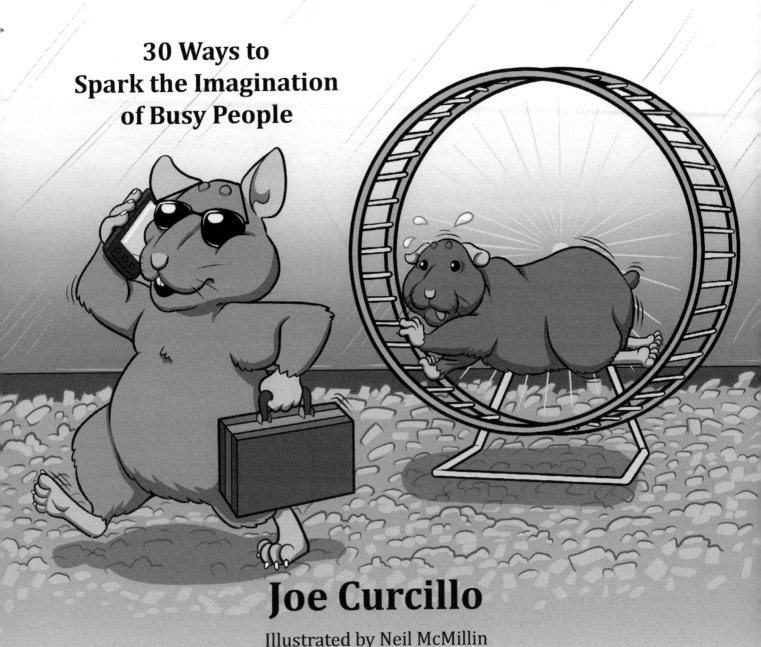

Joe Curcillo

Illustrated by Neil McMillin

This book is dedicated to my eldest daughter, Olivia.
She never told her sister, Kaela, the hamster was gone.

Preface

When my youngest daughter, Kaela, was a child, she had a pet hamster. The hamster's name was Brittany. Brittany was a fluffy brown and white hamster who ate, ran in a wheel, and slept. One day, the hamster wheel stopped spinning. Brittany had escaped.

Realizing that this was a hamster who obviously dreamed of being more than a caged house pet, we allowed her to enjoy her freedom. (No. Not really. We just couldn't find Brittany, so we assumed that she was out chasing her dreams.)

To avoid the inevitable disappointment, I bought an identical hamster and put it in the cage. When Kaela returned home from school, she fed her hamster and went about her homework.

The replacement hamster, "The Hamster," lived out its natural life in its cage. The Hamster lacked vision. It ate, ran in a wheel, and slept. It had no dreams; it was uninspired.

I waited until Kaela was twenty-one to tell her that I had switched hamsters. She is creative. She took it well.

Introduction

Success and creativity live hand-in-hand. Everything we achieve and everything we do begins in our imagination. People imagine they will be successful and then take steps toward success. People imagine that they will win a gold medal or an award, and then they work to achieve those goals.

If we follow the same path as others, we will end up in the same place as everyone else. To forge our own path toward our own personal success, we must create a new way of doing things to discover a new way to stay ahead of the pack. We need to escape the daily grind.

If we want to be more creative than the next person we must allow our imagination to grow to new heights. As we struggle with the day-to-day, our calendars fill up and time becomes scarce. We become stressed over the lack of time, and our ability to exercise our imaginations vanishes. Our brains overload and our dreams disappear.

Without an active imagination we live in a rut, running like a hamster in a wheel. We eat, we sleep, and we get back in the wheel again tomorrow.

In these pages are thirty tips that I developed over thirty years in my dual careers as a trial lawyer and an entertainer. With these tips I have freed up time, I have expanded my horizons, and occasionally, I have found time to sleep. But when you're doing what you love, who wants to sleep?

Many others who have used the thoughts in these pages have, like me, escaped the hamster wheel and found new success. I invite you to join us and open a renewed, vibrant imagination by learning how to manage your time, your thoughts, and your daily life.

With all that said, the simple fact that you're reading this sets you apart from all the other hamsters who are content to stay in the cage. You are clearly not happy with a life of eating, running in the wheel, and sleeping. This book is written for you and for everyone else who is trapped in a hamster wheel yearning to escape, the ones waiting to follow their dreams.

Now is the time to get out of the hamster wheel.

Just imagine...

1. Chase Your Dream

When you are doing something that you enjoy, time flies. The stress of business and work will always be there. But when your dream is on the line, you will not feel the pain of business stress. The joy of being in your happy place will negate the distraction. The more you dream, the more you do. If you follow your goals, you will find that loving what you do increases your ability to be creative and nourishes your imagination. So go chase your dream and enjoy the ride.

Yes, you are busy. But if you chase your dream in small increments, you will move closer to your dream each day.

You can tell this to a hamster, explain that chasing dreams will make it happy, but the hamster will chase nothing. It will eat, run in its wheel, and sleep.

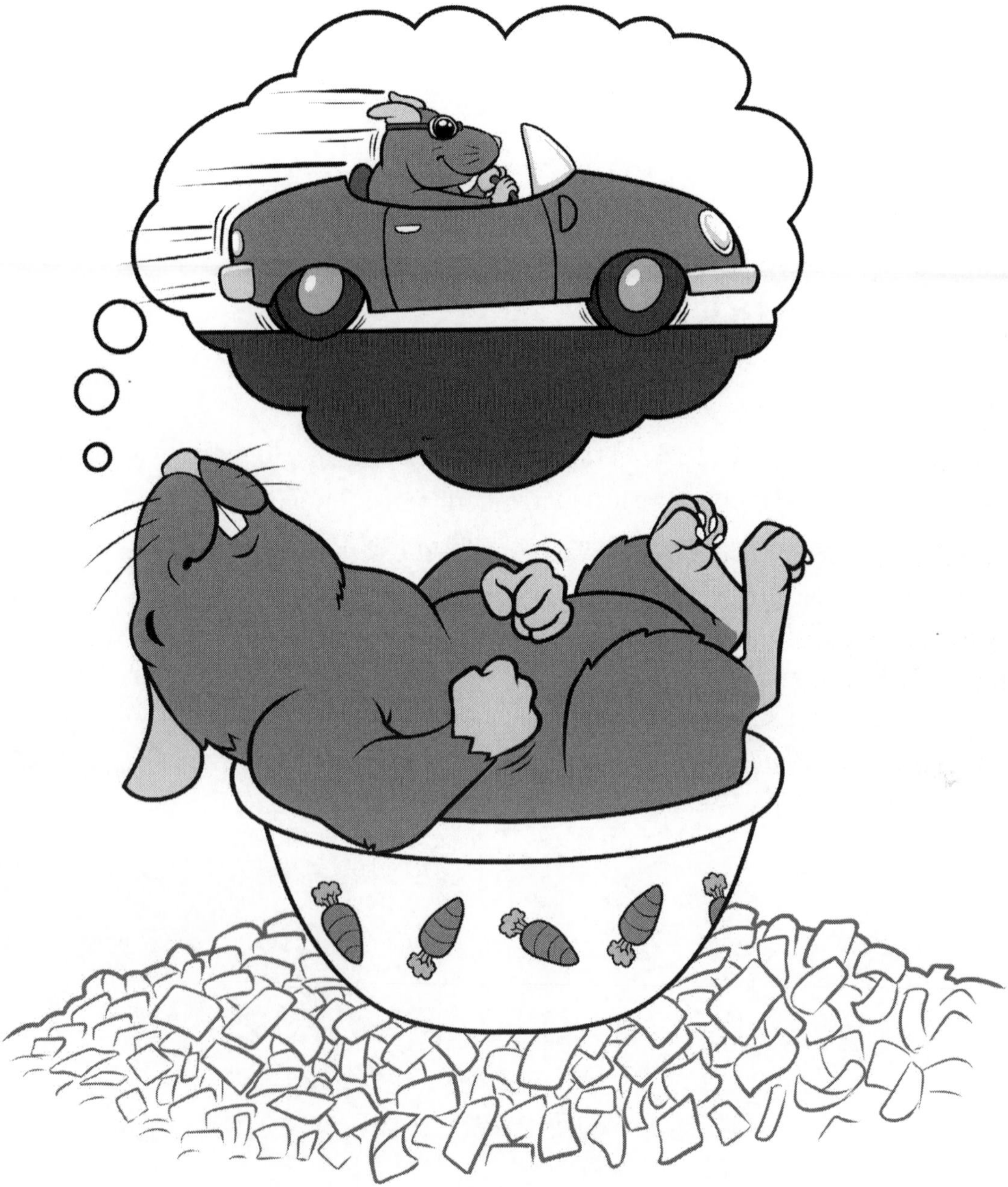

2. Get a Hobby

Find ways to distract yourself from the everyday. Taking up a hobby like collecting antiques, hiking, or playing a musical instrument, will stimulate your imagination. The activities associated with exploring a new hobby will trigger the parts of your brain that thrive on curiosity; you will learn and grow. Along the way, you will unwind and your mind will re-energize, thus revitalizing your thought process. So what will your new hobby be?

You can tell this to a hamster, buy it a guitar, and take it for a walk, but the hamster will eat, run in its wheel, and sleep.

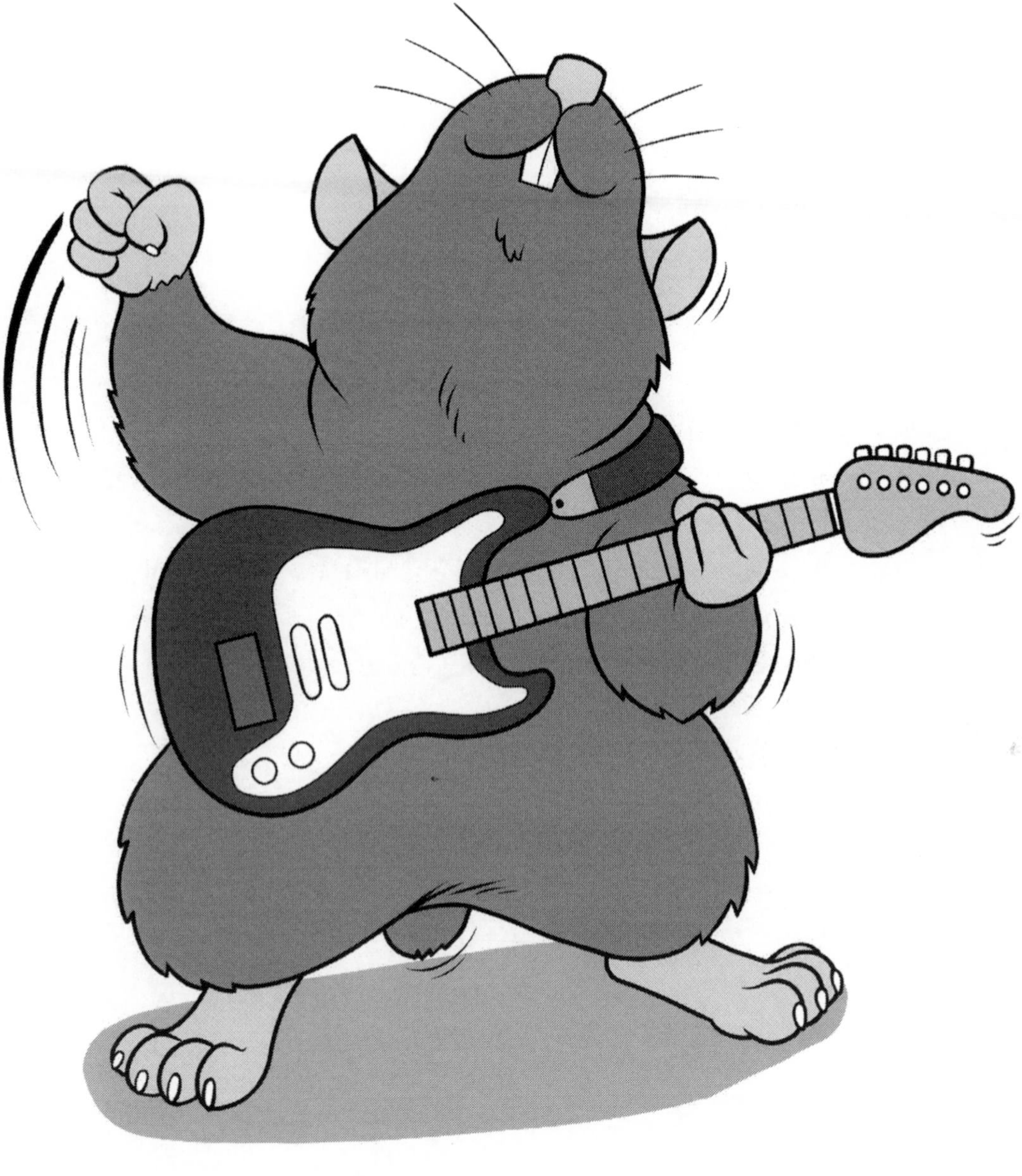

3. Say "No"

Practice saying the word "no." When you are asked to do things for people, think first. Do you really have the time for this? If you don't, politely say "no." Do not feel the least bit guilty. Your time is valuable. You are not rejecting them; you are saving you. Set aside blocks of time during the day to shut off your cell phone and experience *you time.*
If you don't have to answer the phone or reply to a text message, you don't have to say no, because you are avoiding the question without using words.

You can tell this to a hamster, teach it to say "no," and take away its cell phone, but the hamster will eat, run in its wheel, and sleep.

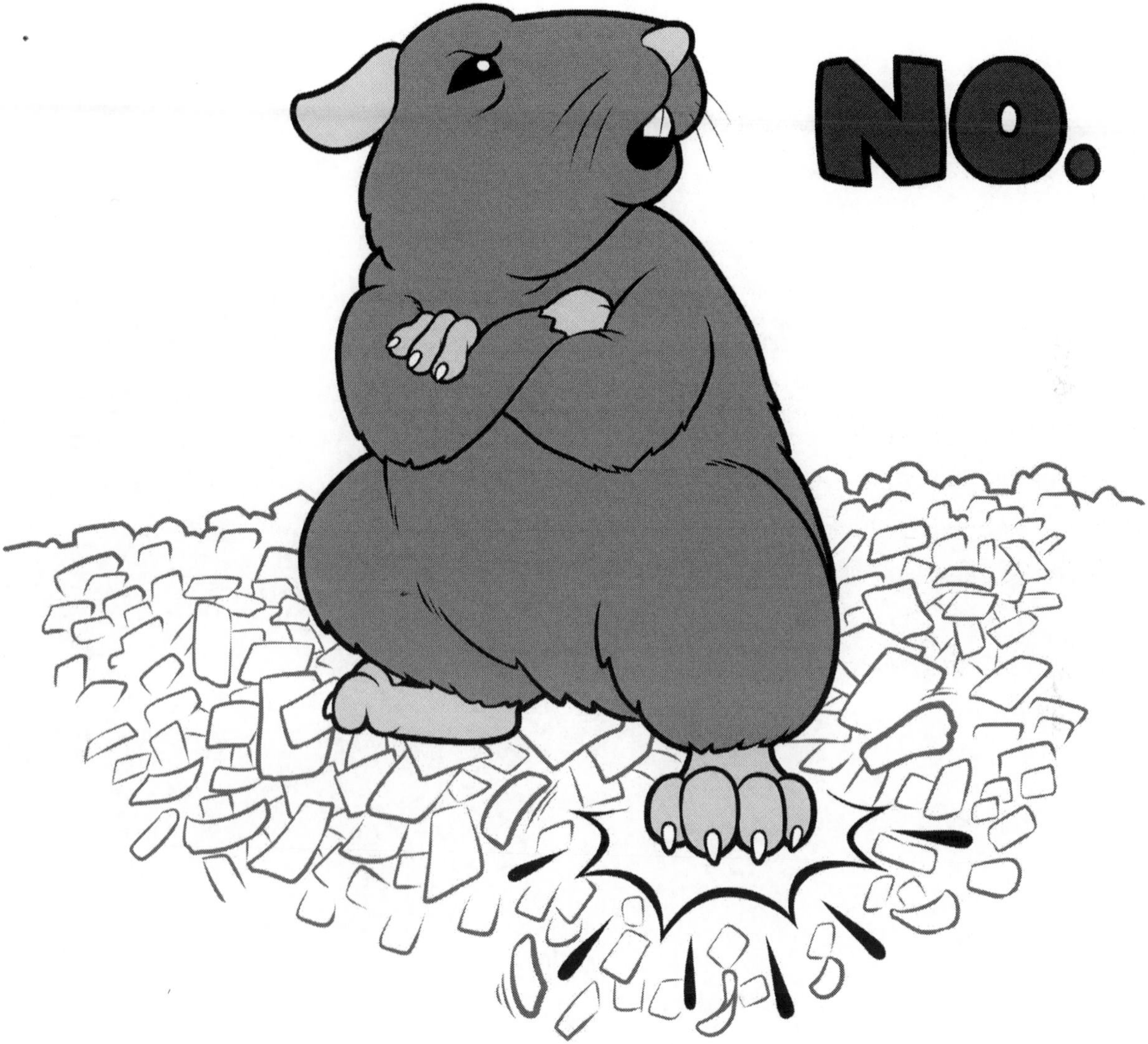
NO.

4. Make a List

Make a to-do list. Write down what you have to do. The written list will clear up prime mental real estate. Keep the list in your phone, hang it on the wall by your desk, or stick it to the refrigerator with a magnetized photo of your cat. But make sure it is visible and handy. Celebrate those moments when you cross off a task. When it comes time to add something to the to-do list, ask yourself if it's important enough to add or if you can forget it. As you write the task, evaluate what should be done soon and what can wait; prioritize the list.

You can tell this to a hamster, buy it a notepad, and put its photo on a refrigerator magnet, but the hamster will eat, run in its wheel, and sleep.

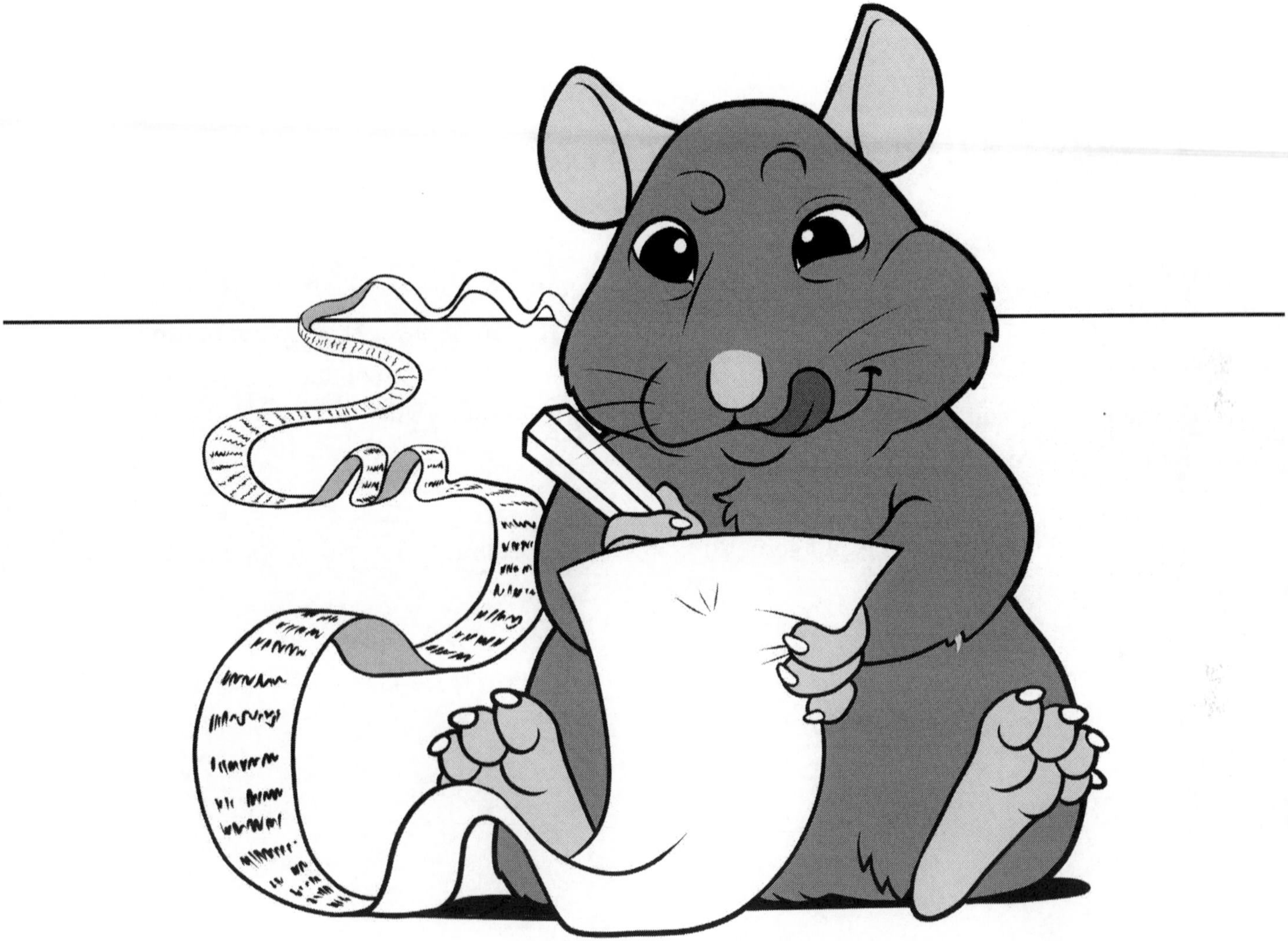

5. Deal with Tough Stuff

When you have something that you really do not want to do, but you know that you must do it, put it on your schedule. Set aside time to finish the task by treating it as an appointment with yourself. Do not miss or postpone the appointment. Once it is scheduled, move on and do not worry about it again until the appointed time. Scheduling the miserable "thing" is liberating. Once it's scheduled, it's half done!

And while you're scheduling, put something fun on your calendar. Keep that appointment too!

You can tell this to a hamster, buy it a calendar, or subscribe it to a reminder service, but the hamster will eat, run in its wheel, and sleep.

6. It's All Noteworthy

Keep a notebook. Don't use your phone; buy an honest-to-God paper notebook. Write down your thoughts when they occur. When an idea comes to you, scribble it in your notebook. You'll be surprised at the number of times during the day when something happens and an idea is born. Most of these ideas die because, within minutes, we're too busy to recall them. If you record your thoughts, you'll remember them at the end of the day.

Today's ideas will feed tomorrow's solutions.

You can tell this to a hamster, buy it a colored marker and a Moleskine notebook, but the hamster will eat, run in its wheel, and sleep.

7. Perfection Is an Excuse

Don't confuse perfectionism with procrastination. Get the task done. If you have something you want to do, it's always best to do it right the first time. But if you define "doing it right" as some kind of unattainable perfection, you are only delaying the inevitable and cluttering your time and thoughts. Do you have to make a phone call that you just can't find the right words to make? Is it because you fear getting a "no?" Make the call now; you will be pleasantly surprised.

You are as perfect as you need to be. You just don't see it.

You can tell this to a hamster, give it encouragement to act immediately, and push it toward the goal, but the hamster will eat, run in its wheel, and sleep.

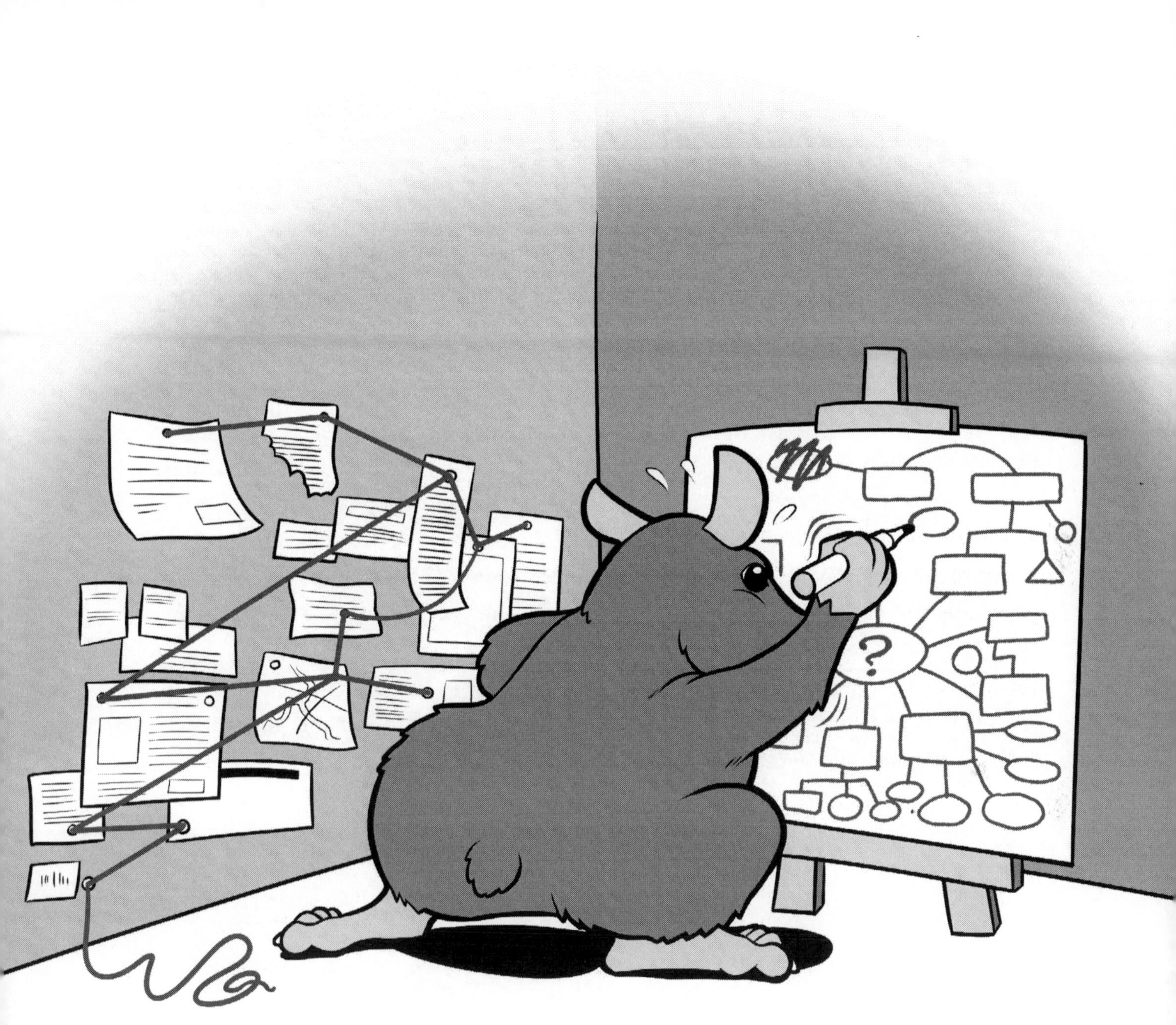

8. Make a Time Plan

Free up your time by scheduling the busy periods in advance. Sit back on a Sunday night and look at your weekly schedule. Look at your to-do list and calendar. Schedule your tasks and phone calls at set times during the week. Evaluate how long you think each task will take and block your time accordingly. This way, the tasks will have definitive start and end times. You will also have the freedom and joy of not worrying about your week, because you know that things are scheduled and ready to go.

You can tell this to a hamster, pour it a glass of wine and hand it a planning calendar, but the hamster will eat, run in its wheel, and sleep.

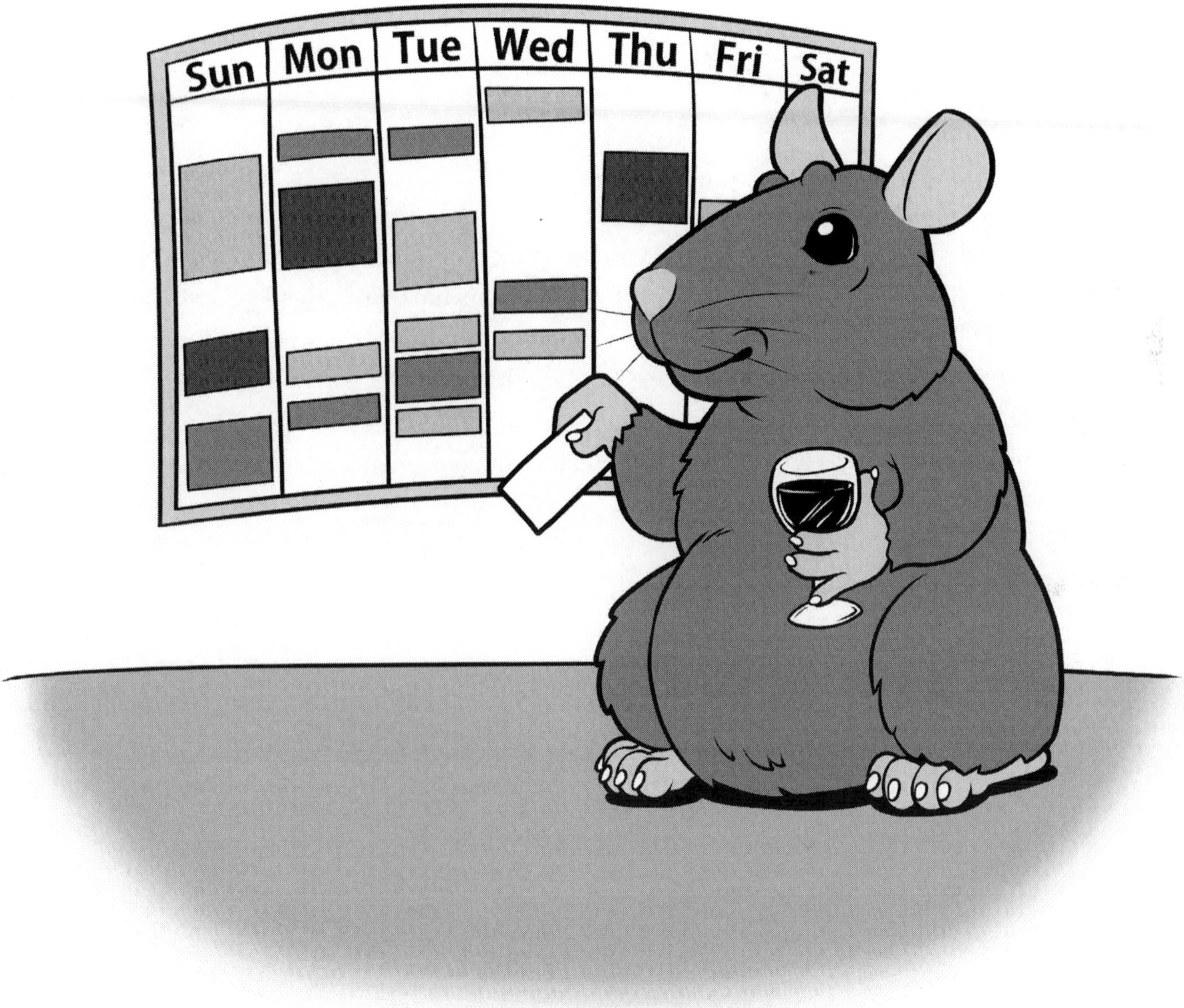
Sun
Mon
Tue
Wed
Thu
Fri
Sat

9. Beat the Clock

When you have an appointment, schedule yourself to be early. Yes, busy people always seem to run late. You are no different. You will probably be late, but if you scheduled yourself to be there early, it's more likely that you will show up on time, and you will be less stressed about a late arrival. This will allow your mind to dive into whatever the appointment is about without carrying the stress of tardiness.

And, if you do arrive early, you'll also have a chance to mingle and network before the scheduled event. Bonus!

You can tell this to a hamster, give it an iWatch or a kitchen timer, but the hamster will eat, run in its wheel, and sleep.

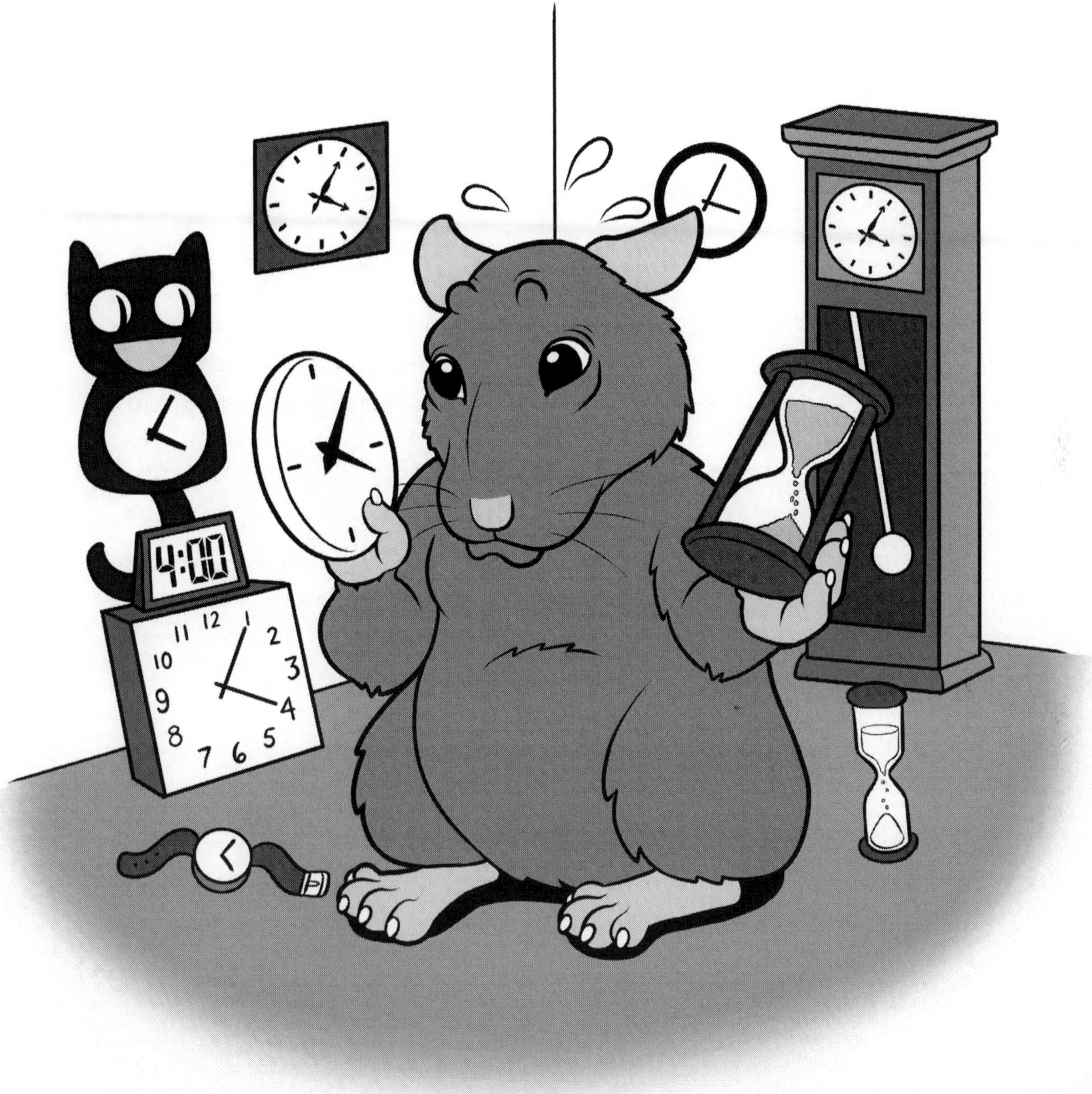
4:00

10. Buffer zones

When you schedule appointments, create buffer zones. Give yourself time between each appointment to process what you did in the last appointment and reflect upon what you are going to do in the next. Without this practice, your appointments will run back to back and you will forget some of the more important thoughts that occur to you both before and after the busy periods.

This time can be spent in a coffee shop, at your desk, or in your car. The location doesn't matter. Just breathe.

You can tell this to a hamster, take it to your favorite coffee shop to chill over a croissant, but the hamster will eat, run in its wheel, and sleep.

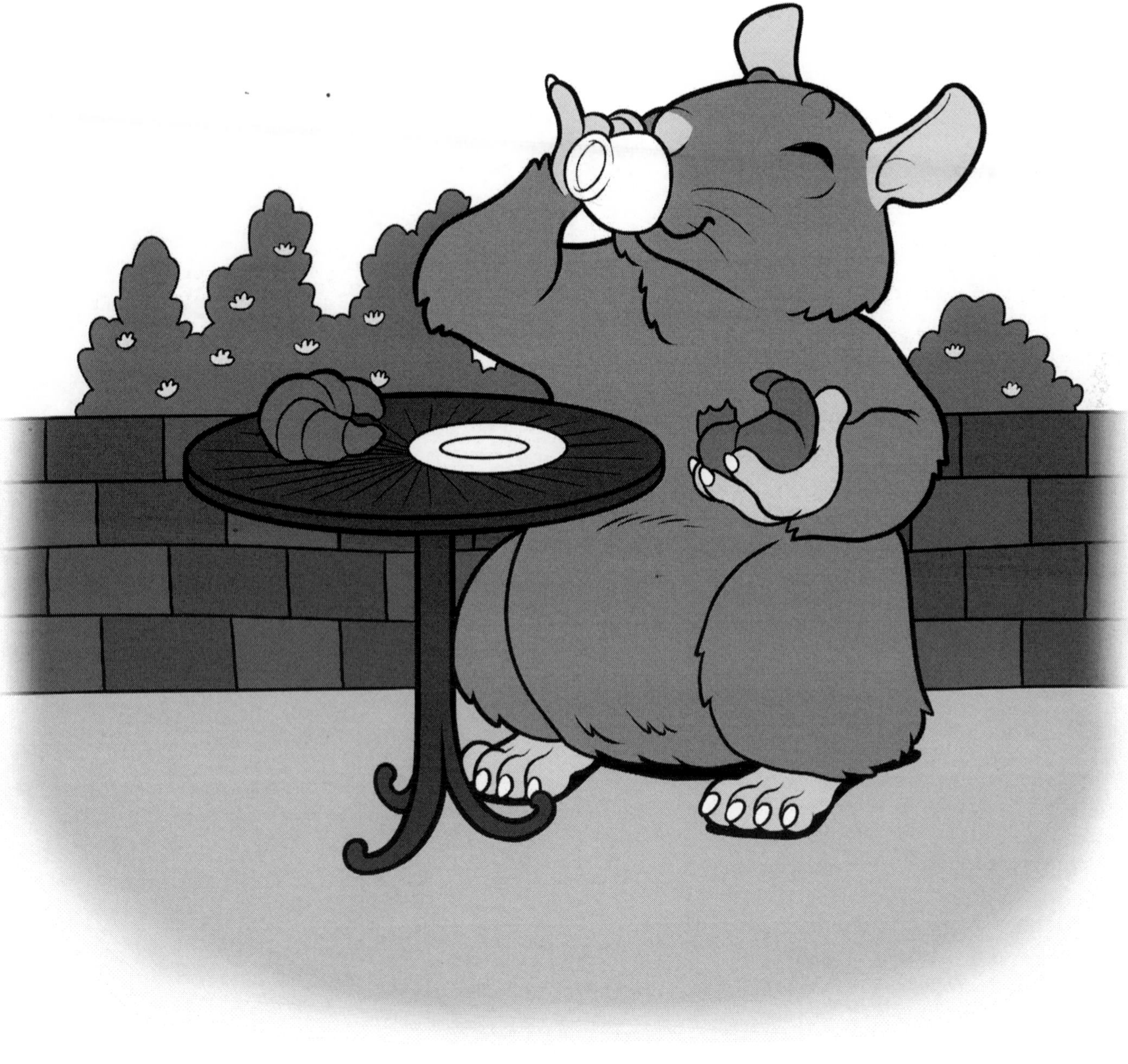

11. Create a Fun Space

Surround yourself with things that make you happy. The environment in which you work will, for better or worse, be reflected in your efforts. If you work in an office that is sterile and boring, you will produce sterile and boring work. If your office is adorned with things that make you smile and be happy, you will produce things that make you—and others—smile and be happy. As children, we were excited to be surrounded by our toys.
Just because you grew up doesn't mean it's time to stop.

You can tell this to a hamster, surround it with a chew toy and pictures of its 432 offspring, but the hamster will eat, run in its wheel, and sleep.

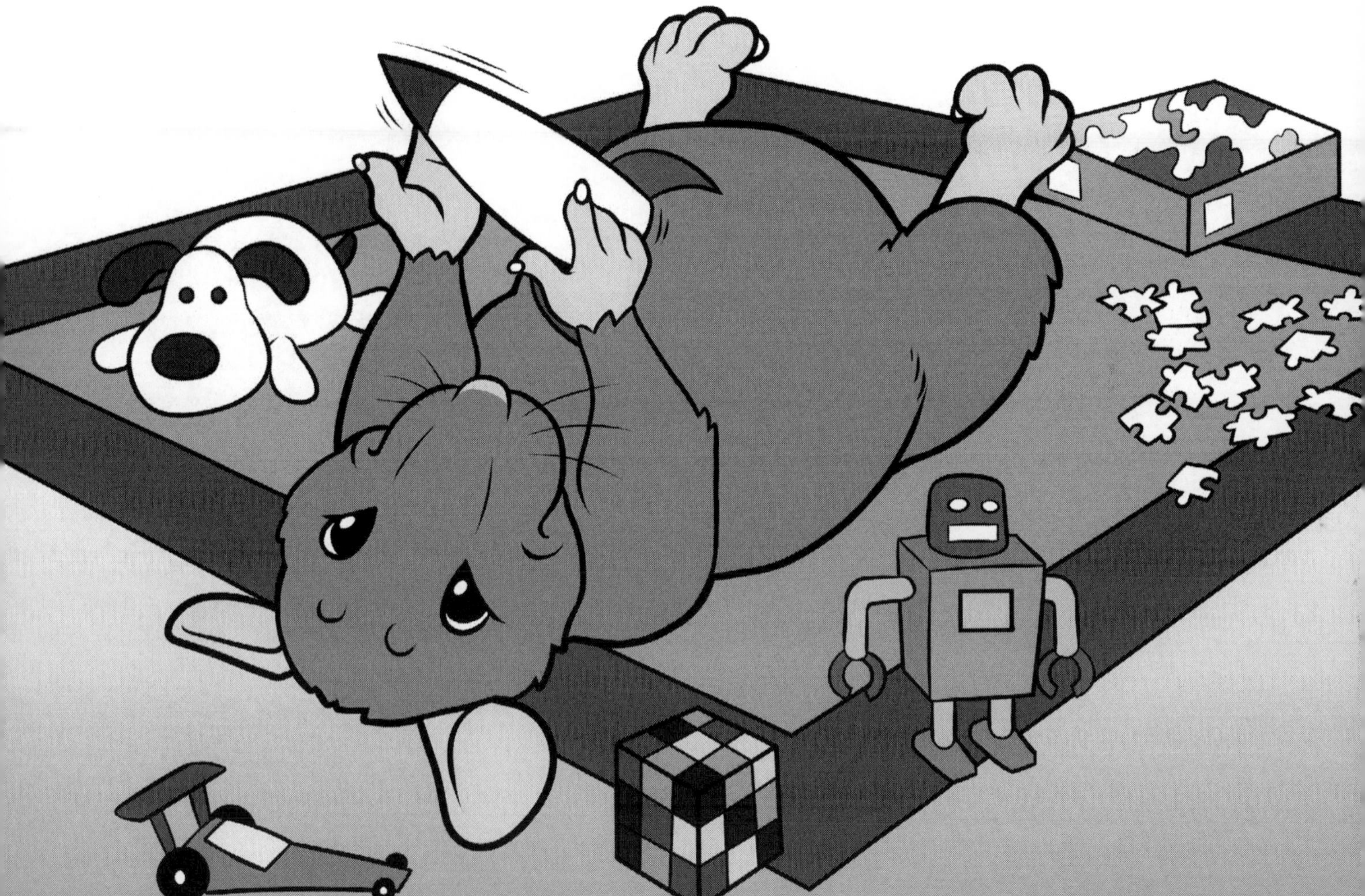

12. Make Something

Maybe you will find happiness by joining a pottery class, making wine in your home, or doodling the evening away. Be creative in all that you do. When you take a few moments to involve yourself in a creative task, you tend to focus more on that task than on the all-consuming busyness of day-to-day life. Make something that you will see completed in a definite window of time. The feeling of accomplishment when you have finished a drawing, or when you taste something that you just cooked from a new recipe, will inspire you to do new things more often. Your relaxed mind will be more productive.

You can tell this to a hamster, give it a jar of Play-Doh and a belt sander, but the hamster will eat, run in its wheel, and sleep.

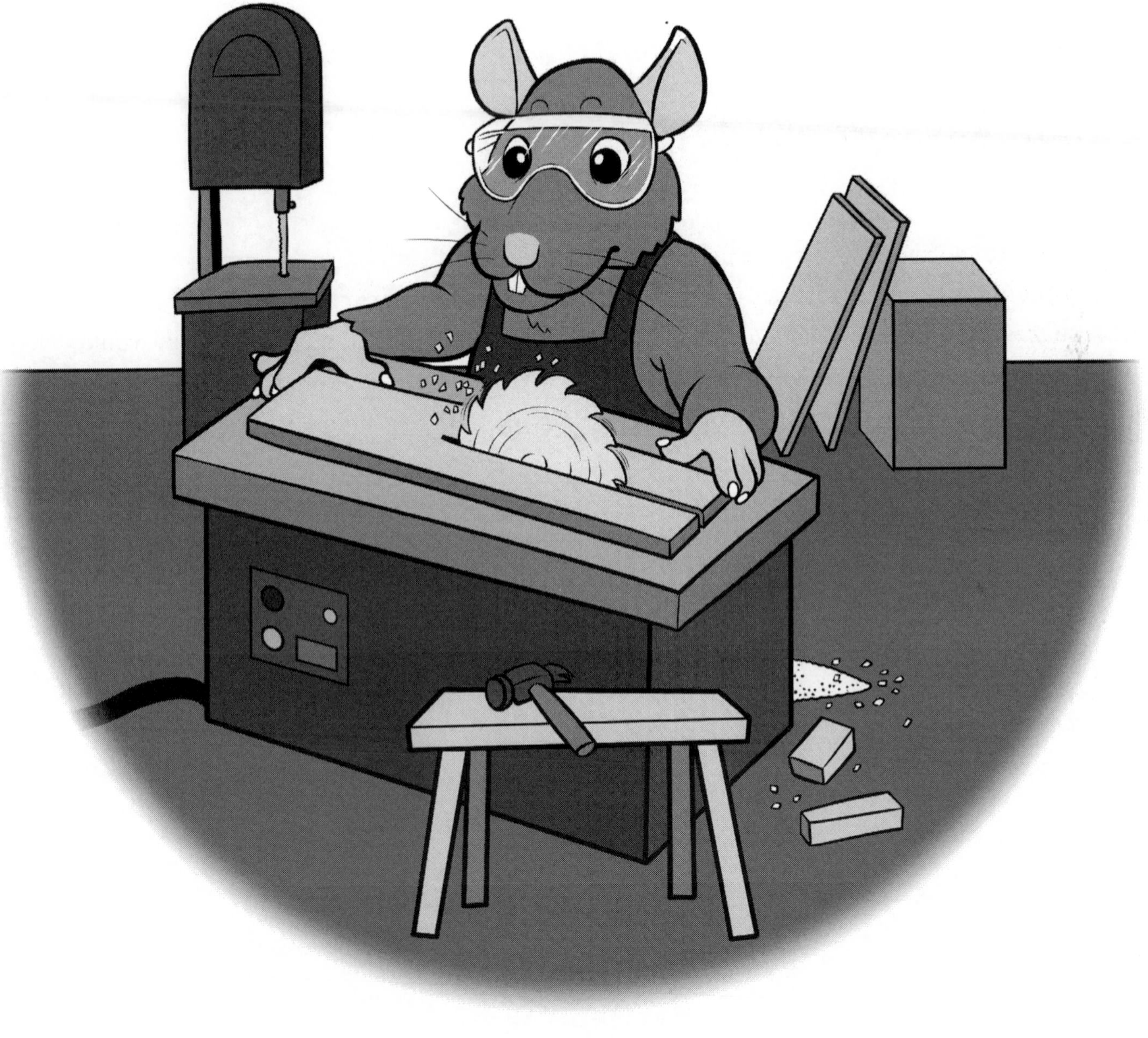

13. Do Something

Decide to do something you've never done before. Look at your bucket list and ask yourself: Is there something that I have been wanting to do that I can learn to do now? I'm not suggesting that you go out and bungee jump or learn to fly an airplane, though they would be good exhilarating things to do. Your mind can be exhilarated by simply taking a tai chi class, going on a long-awaited trip, or visiting your long-lost rich uncle in Tulsa.

You can tell this to a hamster, take it to the top of the St. Louis Arch with a rubber-band bungee, but the hamster will eat, run in its wheel, and sleep.

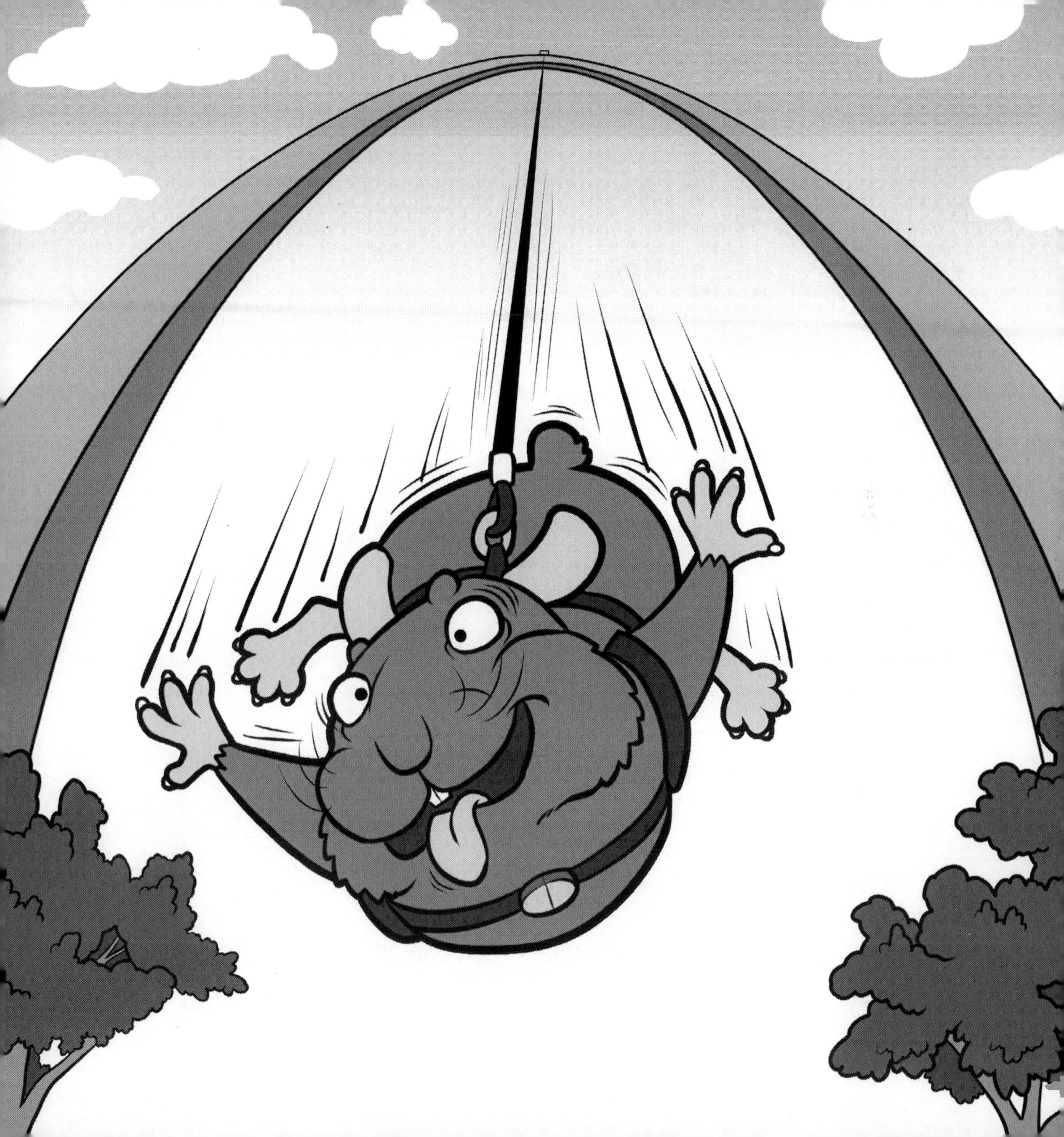

14. Open Your Mind

Force yourself to come up with brave new ideas. Shake your fears. Consider new things to do in your business or your personal life. See if you can come up with new ways of accomplishing a task. Look up an old recipe, change the ingredients, and come up with something new. Don't worry about how it's going to taste, you will find out soon enough. I once took apart an entire computer system just to see if I could put it back together. I was successful, and I learned that the computer manufacturer obviously used three more screws than they needed. I threw the screws away and the computer worked fine. Explore!

You can tell this to a hamster, challenge it to come up with an original idea, but the hamster will eat, run in its wheel, and sleep.

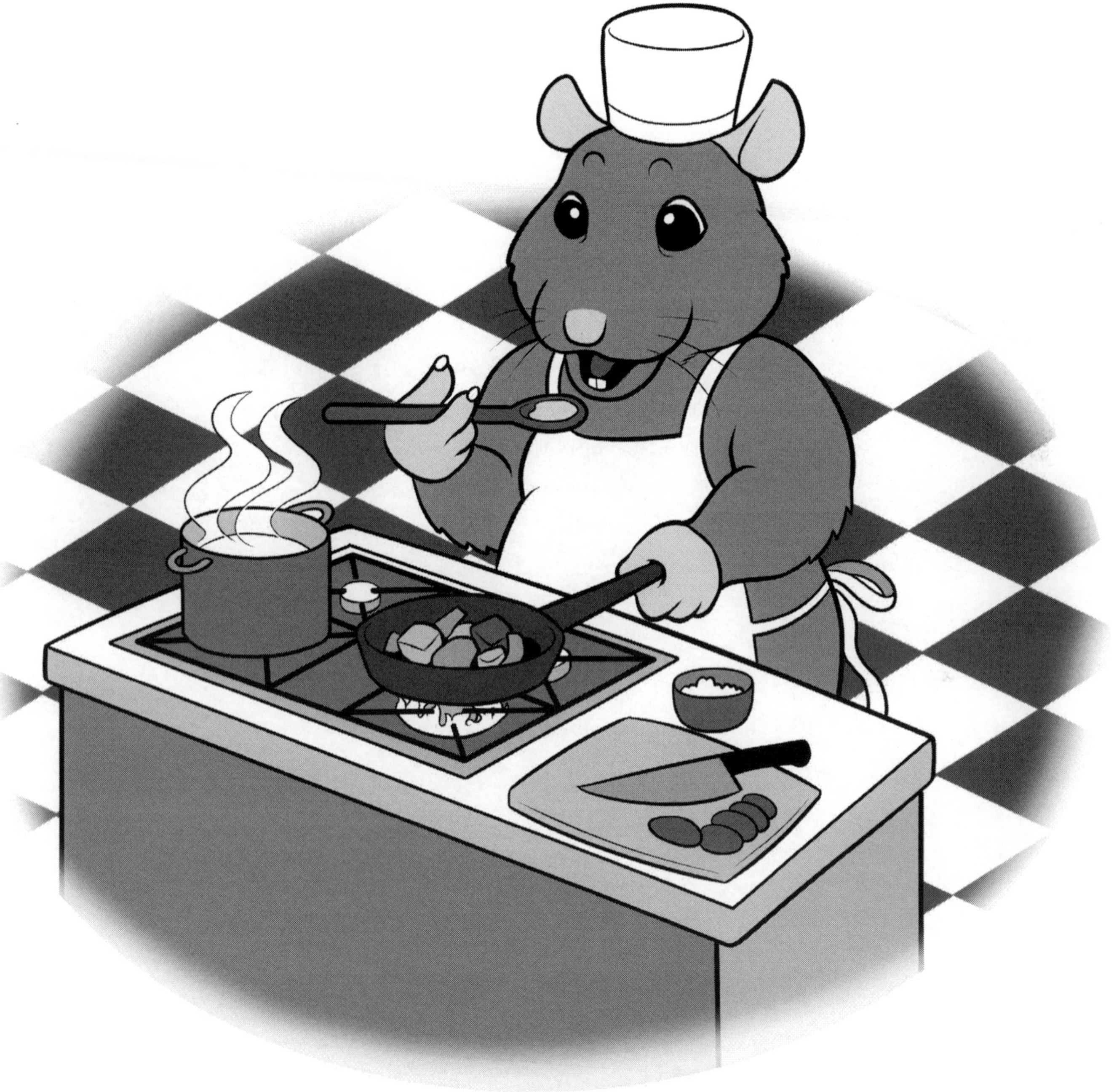

15. Talk in Color

When someone asks you how your day is, don't just say good. Visualize your day. Give them an answer that allows them to visualize the high points. When you encourage your mind to be descriptive, you increase your imagination. Even if you do not share all the minute details, imagine the story in living color. The more elaborate and detailed your descriptions, the more inspired your imagination will become. Don't just tell a story. Recall the visuals of the location, describe what you heard, and maybe even how things smelled. For example, if it occurred on a cruise ship, incorporate the rocking of the boat and the scent of the salt air into your story. Don't be satisfied with the plain and the unadorned. Make it real.

You can tell this to a hamster, place it in a story circle surrounded by a room of eager listeners, but the hamster will eat, run in its wheel, and sleep.

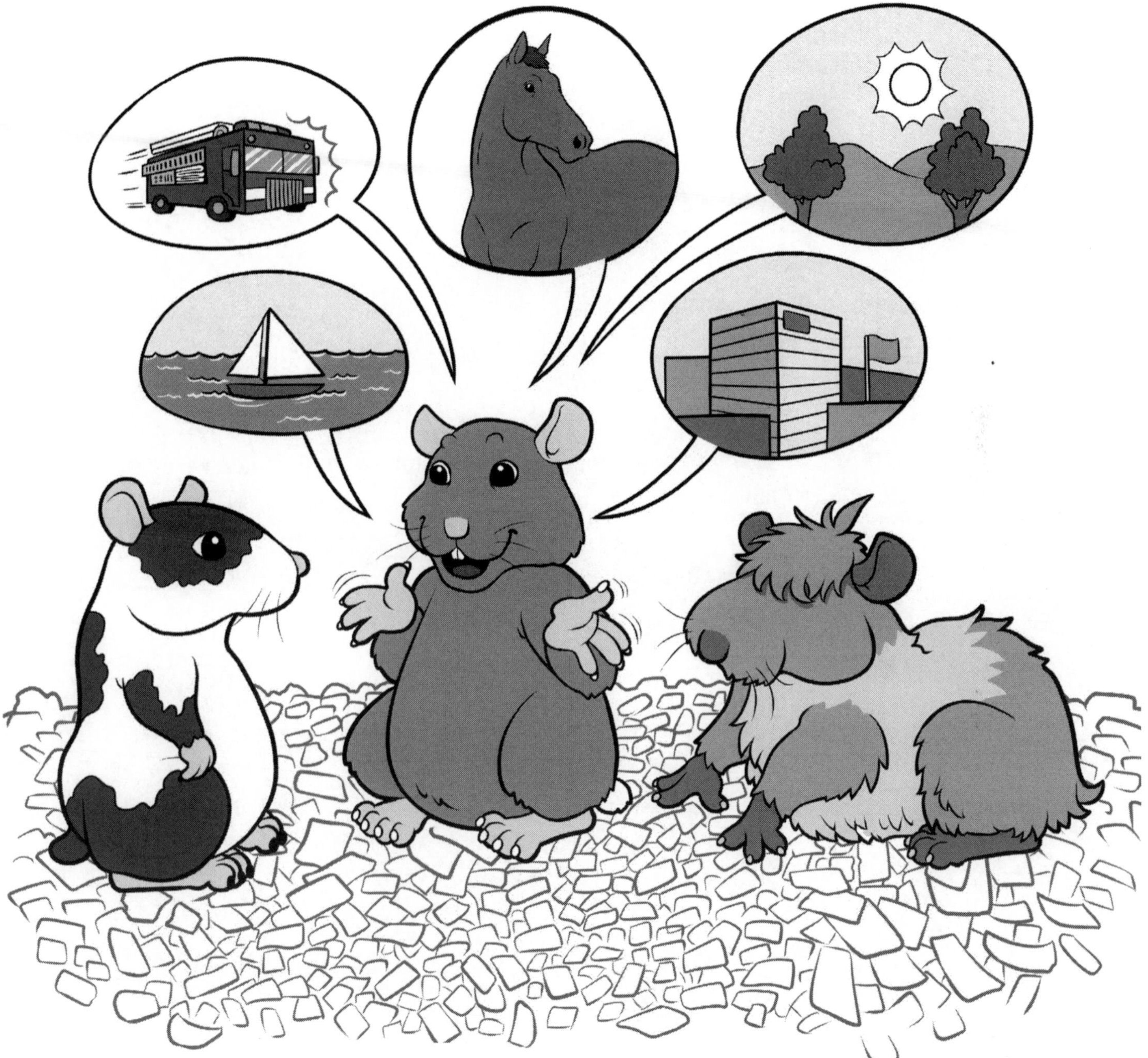

16. Learn Something

We have all developed a talent. You may not recognize it is a talent, but we all have something that we have learned to do well. Pick a new talent. Choose something that you already have an interest in but have never tried. Always be ready to learn new things. The more you seek answers and try to learn something new, the more your curiosity and imagination thrive. As we get older and busier, we tend to stop learning. When we do that, our minds stop growing. Challenge yourself to set sail toward a new adventure in learning.

You can tell this to a hamster, take it to a swimming pool to learn to swim, but the hamster will eat, run in its wheel, and sleep.

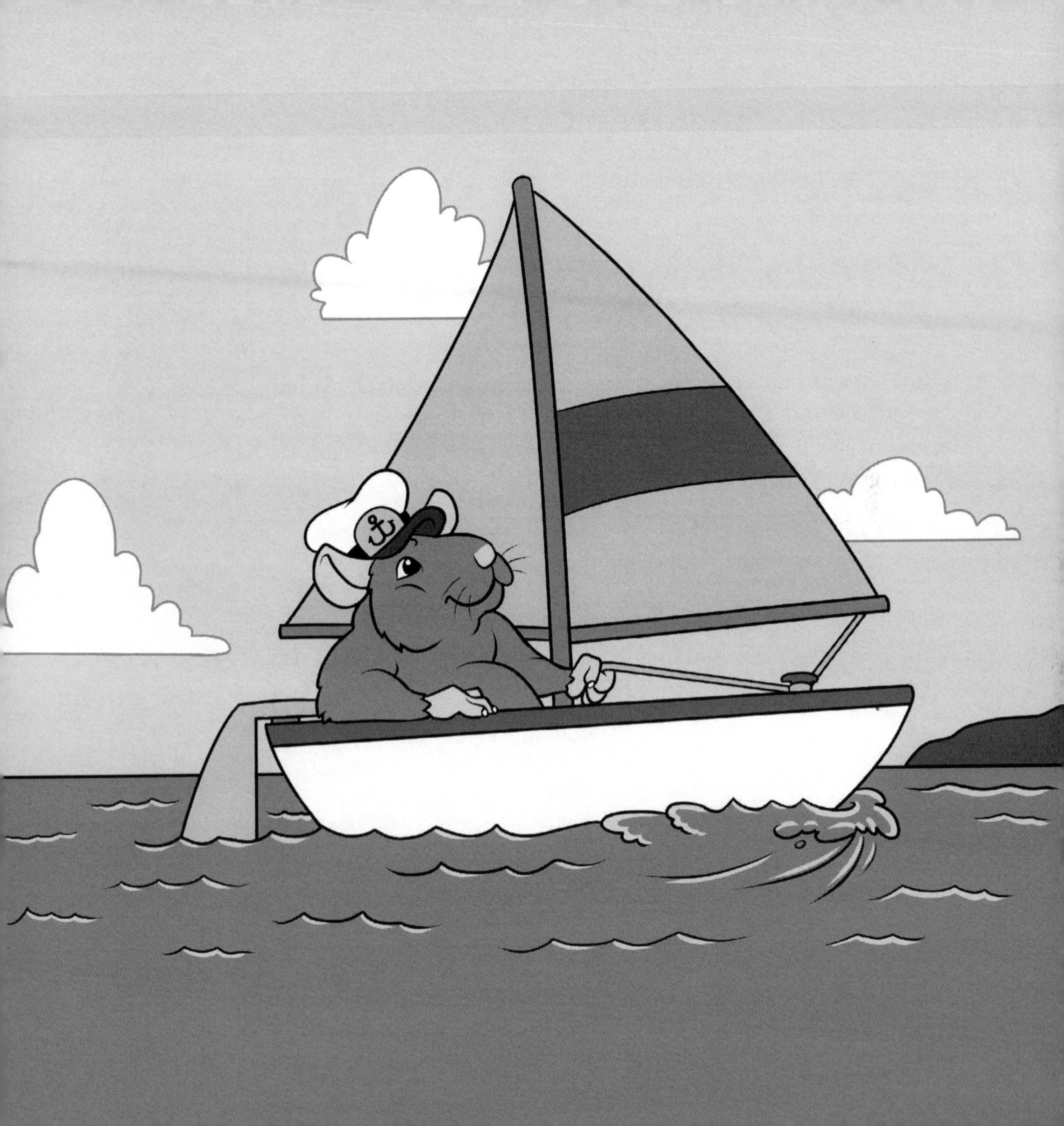

17. Make Creative Friends

Hang out with creative people. Maybe it's joining a book club. Or maybe it's joining a theater company. Maybe it's hanging out with a bunch of geeks. It doesn't matter what group of people you choose so long as they share your interest and create an opportunity for you to learn more. Just talking to people and brainstorming with them will get your creative energies flowing in new directions.

How you choose to spend your free time, and who you choose to spend it with, will alter your perspective for better or for worse. Choose wisely.

You can tell this to a hamster, take it to the improv, and introduce it to your friends, but the hamster will eat, run in its wheel, and sleep.

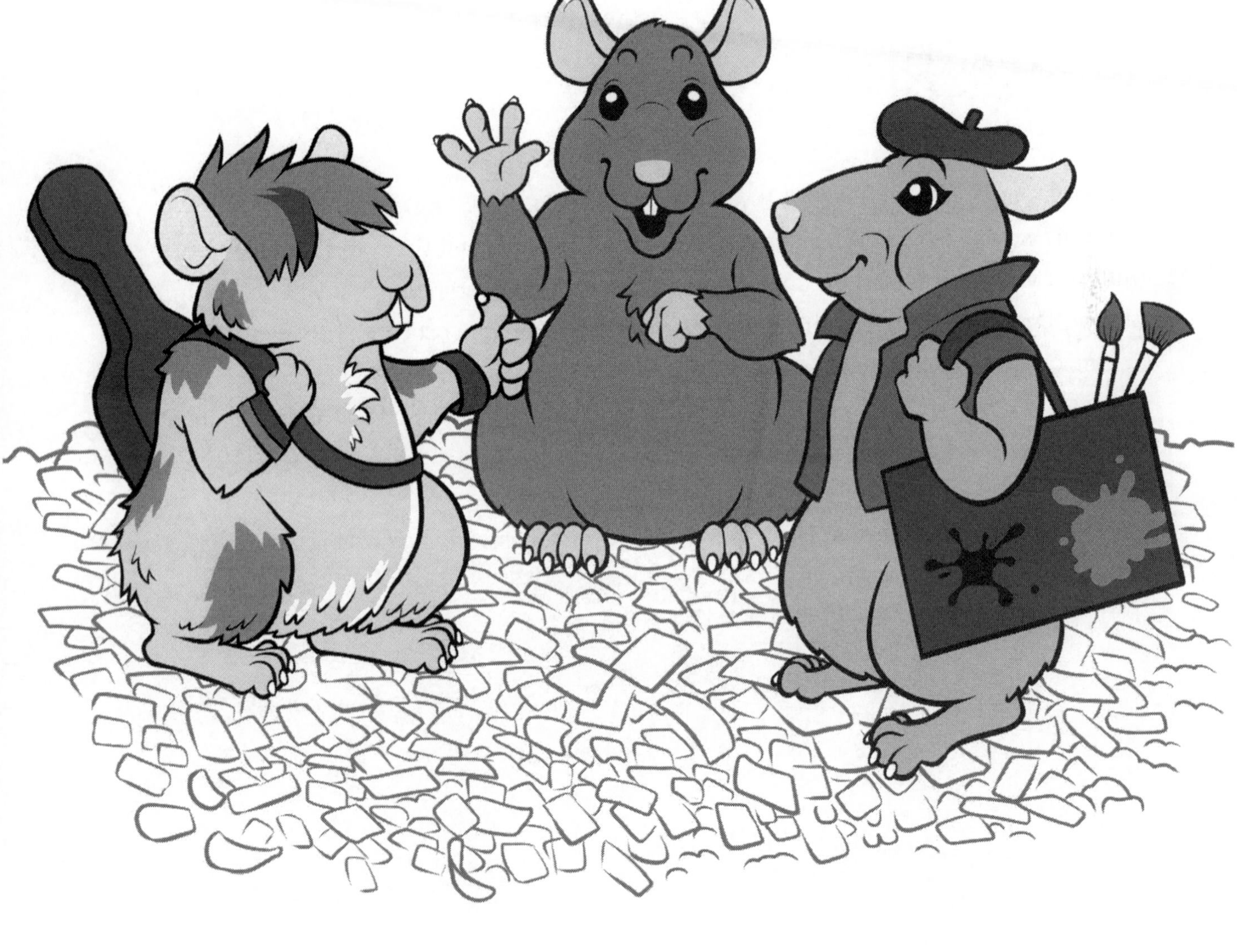

18. See Differently

Break up your ordinary routine. If you always take the same route to work, choose a different way and see new things on your drive. When you get tired and bored, take a different view of the world around you and create a new perspective. If you do a mundane task at the office every morning, do it differently. Change the order, change the pattern of action, or change the color of ink in your pen; change *something!* A fresh, original approach will give your mind a jolt. Creativity and imagination will flourish when you step away from the ordinary routine.

You can tell this to a hamster, put it in a whole new cage next to a new window, but it will eat, run in its wheel, and sleep.

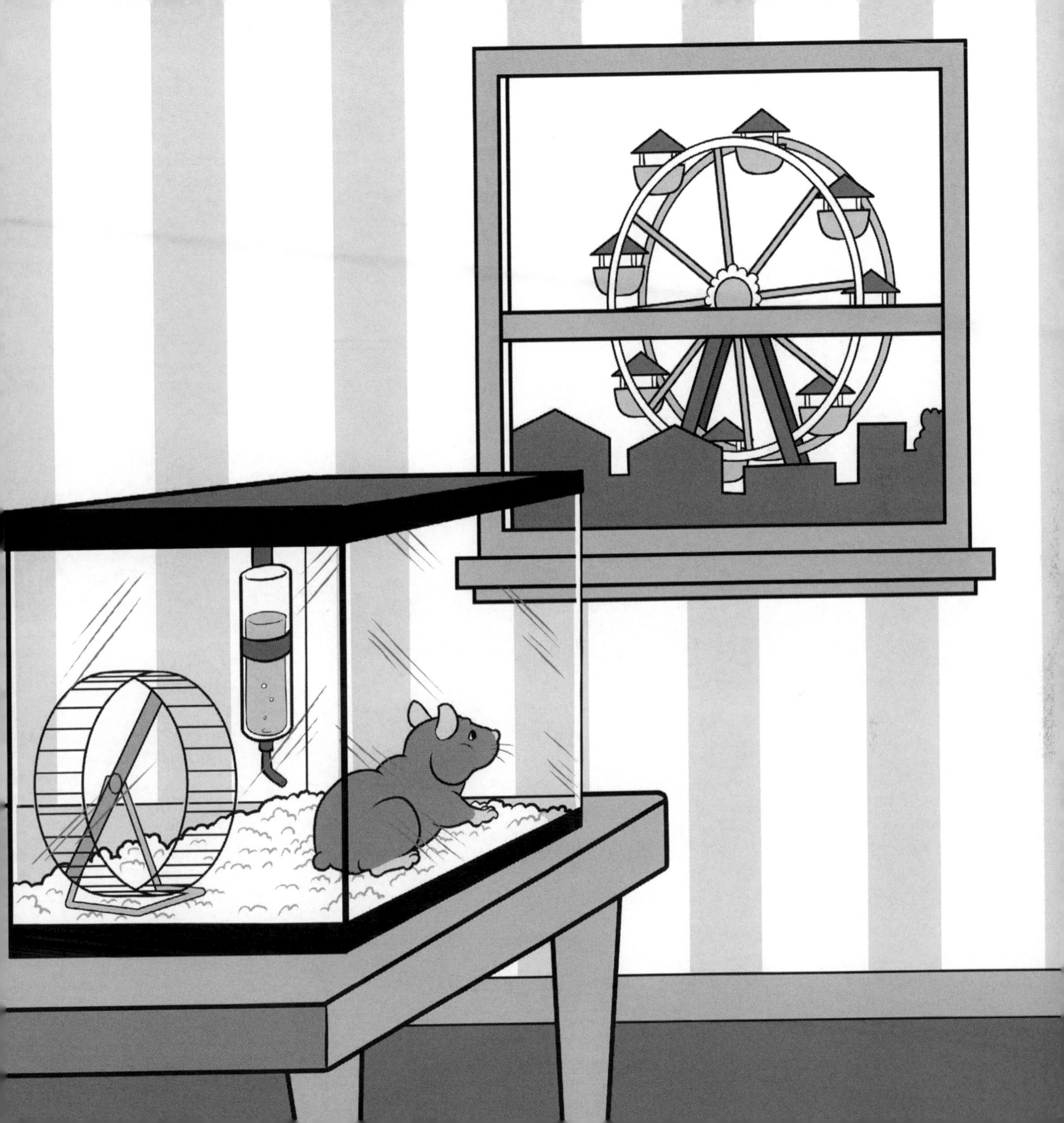

19. Meditate

Take time to relax your mind. Find a quiet place, sit in silence, or turn on soothing music, and think of nothing. Yes, it's hard to clear your mind of all things, but if you sit still and listen intently to the sounds around you, or focus on each note of the music, your brain will relax and clear, and then it will reach new levels of activity. Consider the quiet time as a tune-up for your brain. Go, meditate, be present, and refresh your mind.

You can tell this to a hamster, play a little Rachmaninoff in the background, and put it on a soft pillow, but it will eat, run in its wheel, and sleep.

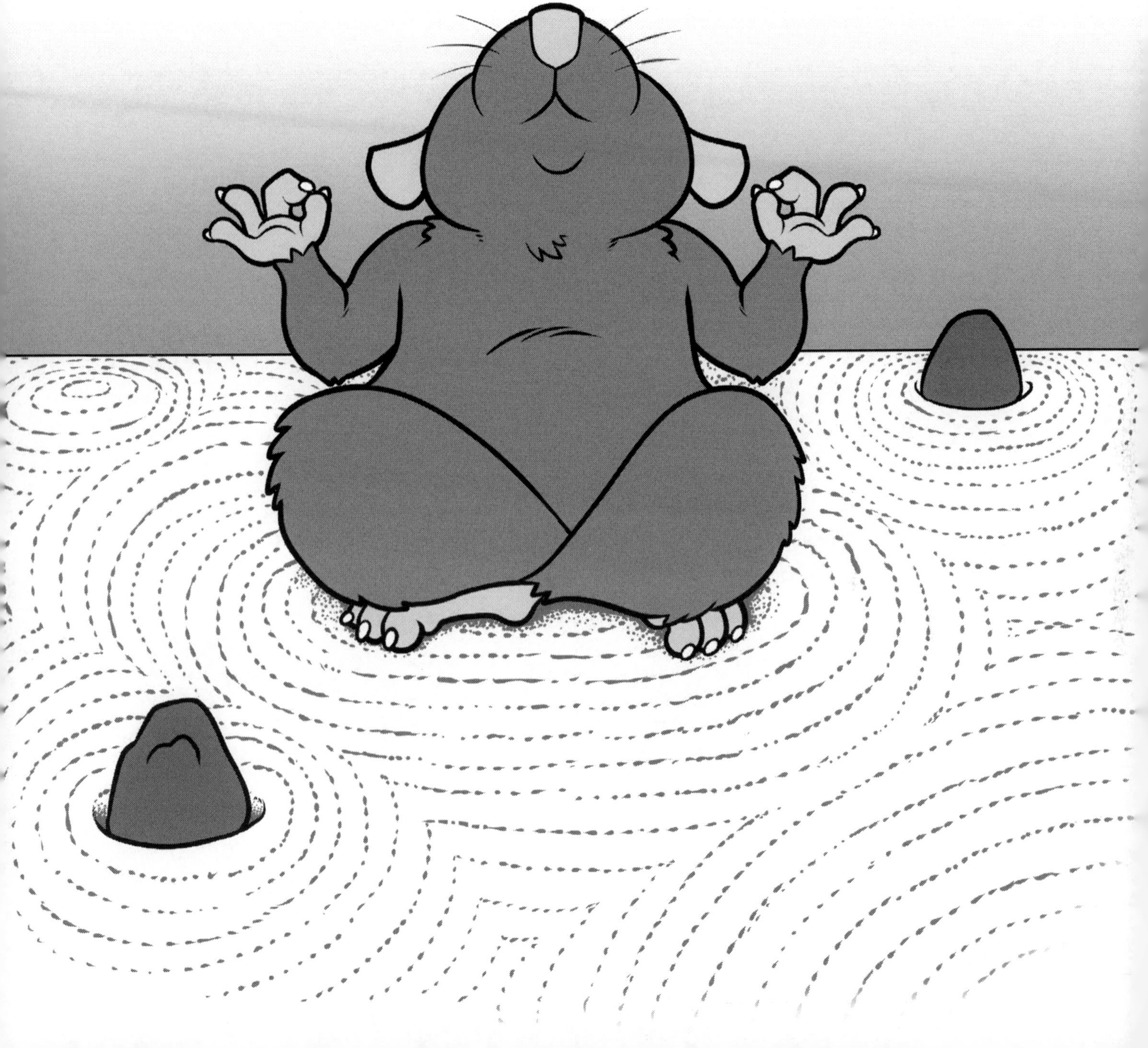

20. Take a Nap

A nap is sometimes the best way to walk away from a problem. Whenever you face a difficult or stressful task, your mind goes on overload. Step away and take a power nap. It might be the greatest reboot your thoughts have ever had. Sometimes, when the stress gets us, we pull all-nighters to solve the problem. This will wear down your ability to see clearly. There is nothing like a power nap to awaken an imaginative solution.

You can tell this to a hamster, but it won't give your advice a second thought. It will eat, run in its wheel, and sleep.

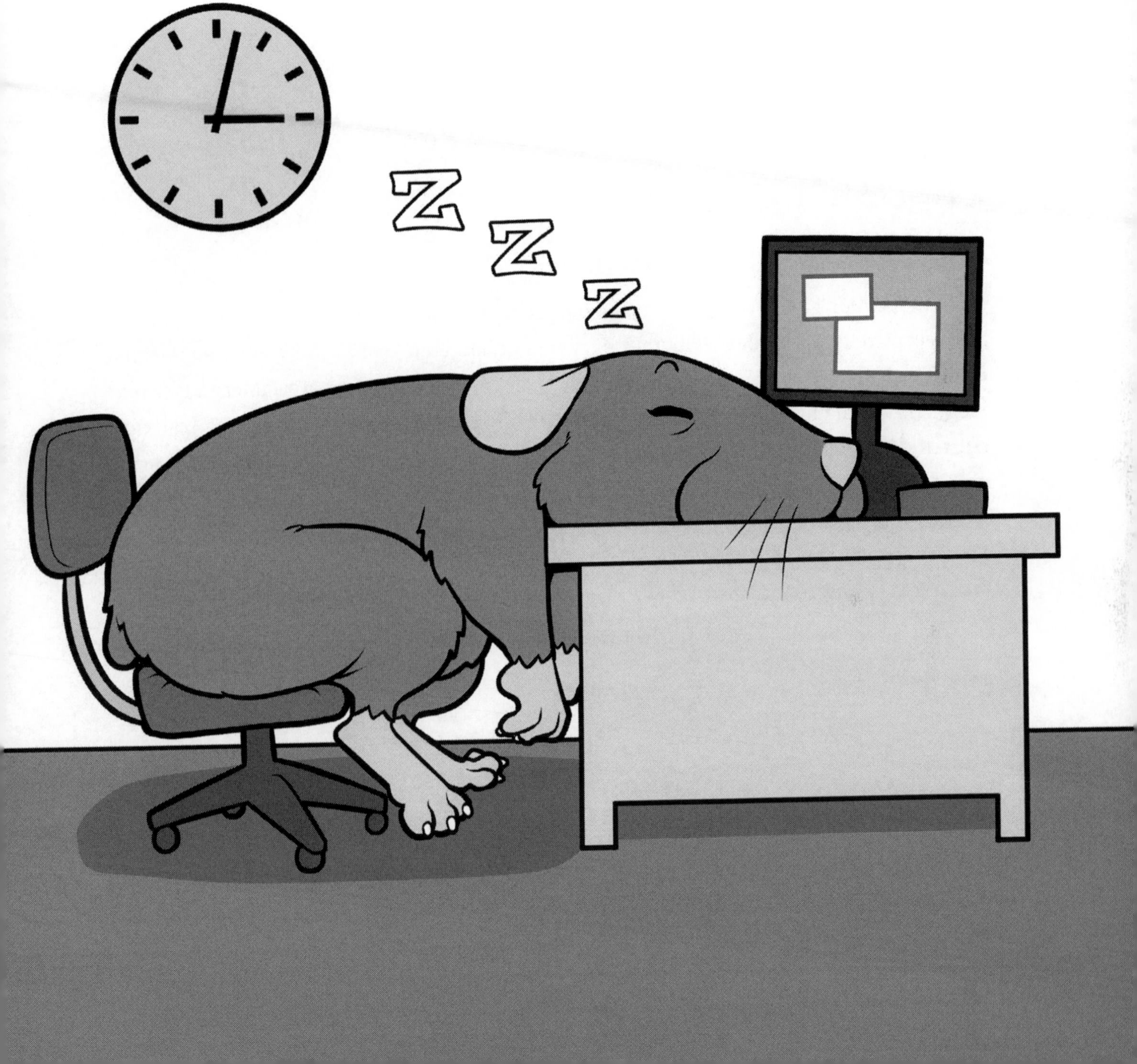
Z
Z
Z

21. Don't Judge

Don't judge. Don't let your own personal biases get in your way. Keep your mind open and receptive to every idea—whether it's yours or someone else's. The minute you begin to criticize an idea, forward motion stops. Opinions stop the flow of creative energy. Passing judgment on an idea is like putting a cotton shirt into a washing machine on hot. Like the shirt, the imagination shrinks and becomes constraining. Explore all possibilities with enthusiasm and keep your ideas growing!

You can tell this to a hamster, and wait for its opinion, but you will not get one because the hamster is predisposed to eat, run in its wheel, and sleep.

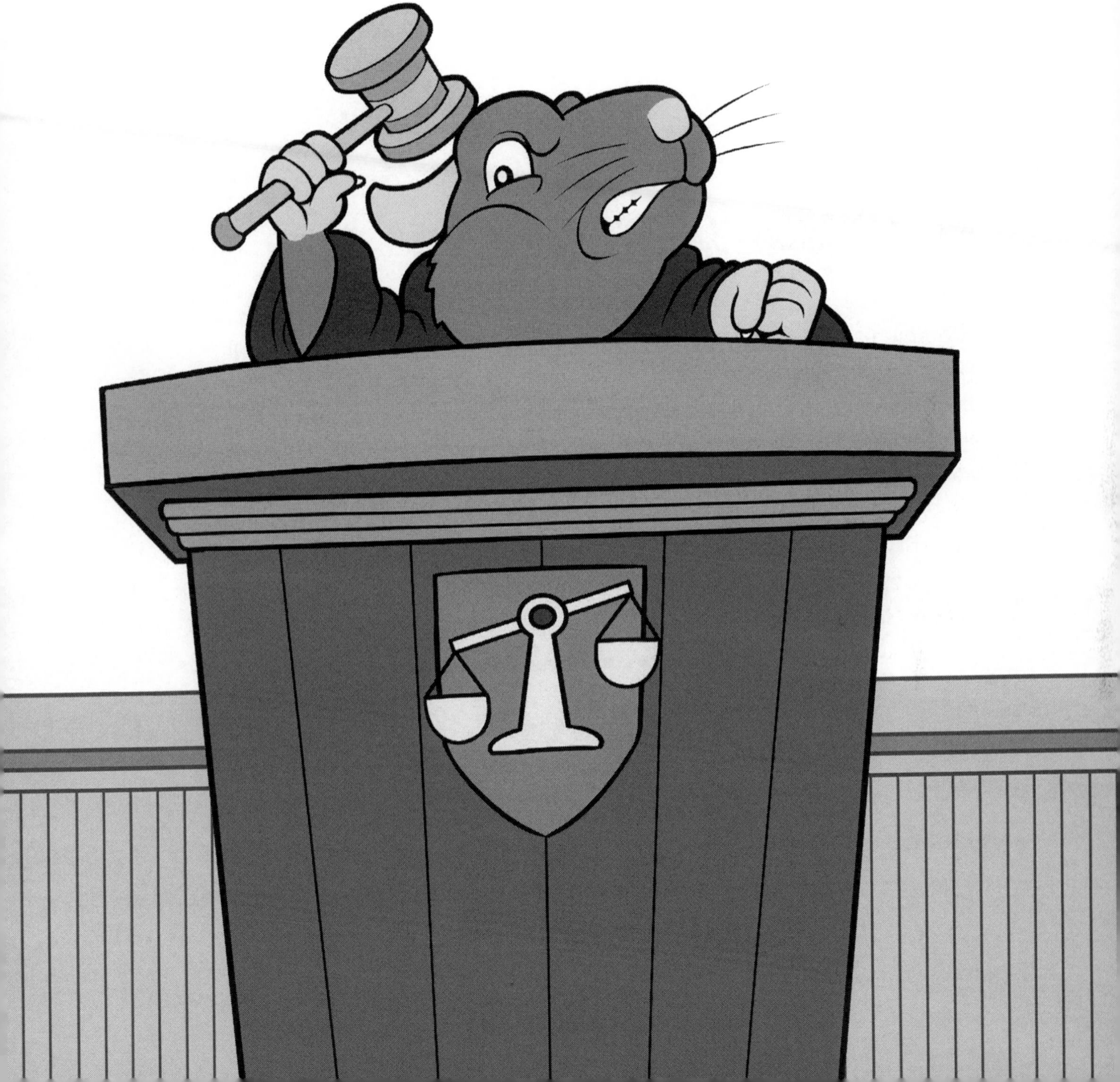

22. Obsess, Obsess, Obsess

Love your passion. Devour your passion. Let your passion totally consume you. The more you obsess over your passion, the more it will readily take over your dreams and your day-to-day life. The more you think about that which empowers and excites you, the more you will explore new possibilities. When this happens, your imagination will run rampant, and new ideas will become your obsession.

Strive to develop expertise in all that you are passionate about!

You can tell this to a hamster, but the hamster will not get excited; it will only do what it knows how to do: eat, run in its wheel, and sleep.

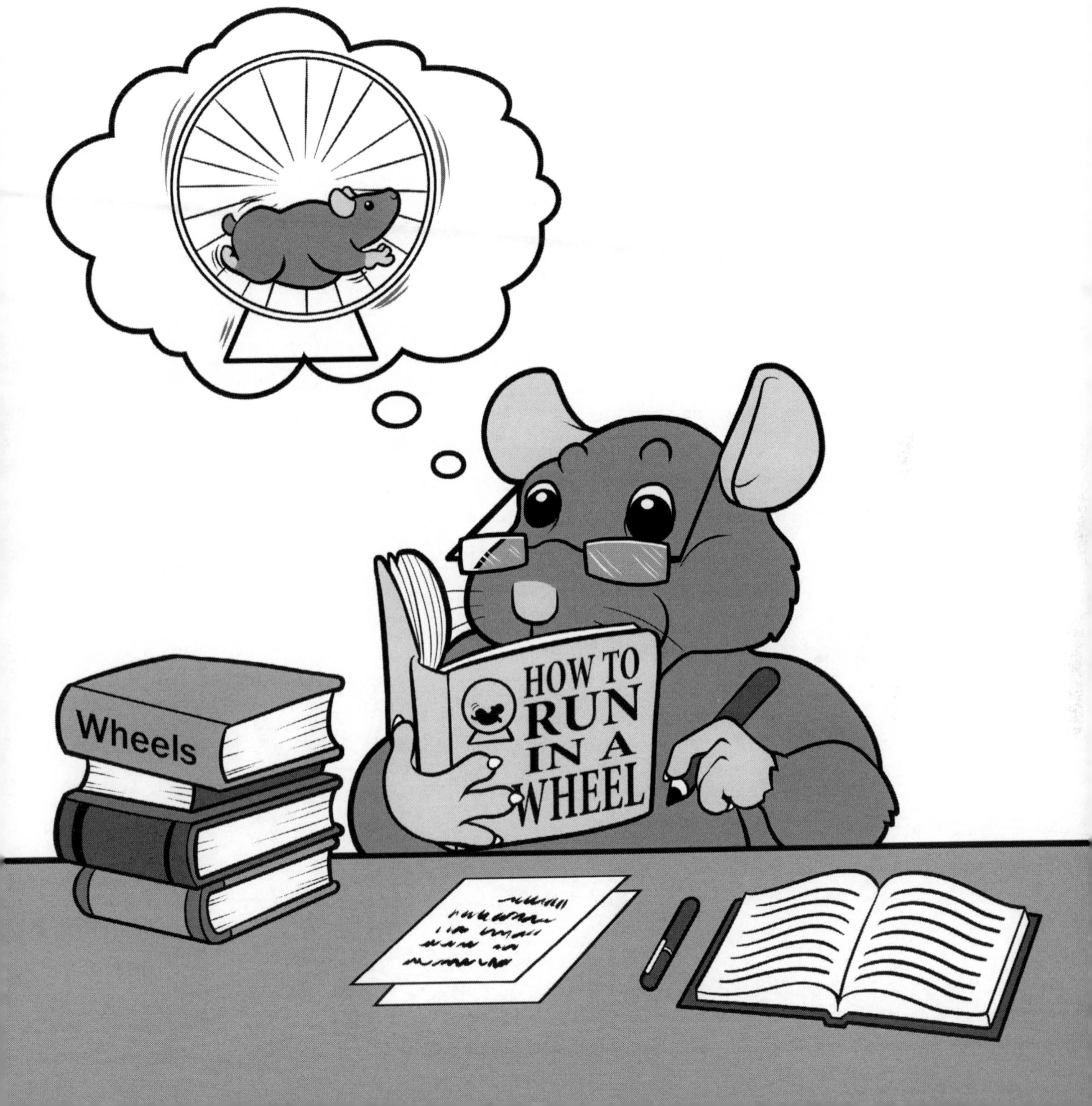
Wheels
HOW TO RUN IN A WHEEL

23. Think in Pictures

We all use words to think and communicate. The more visual your words the more you can see what you're thinking. Visualizing your thoughts creates a whole new experience. When you speak, visualize the pictures that go with the words. See future events in pictures as real as those you can see from the past. The details you imagine will take root in your thoughts. Visually imagine your thoughts; they will become real.

You can tell this to a hamster, but the hamster will stare back at you through the bars of its cage, then eat, run in its wheel, and sleep.

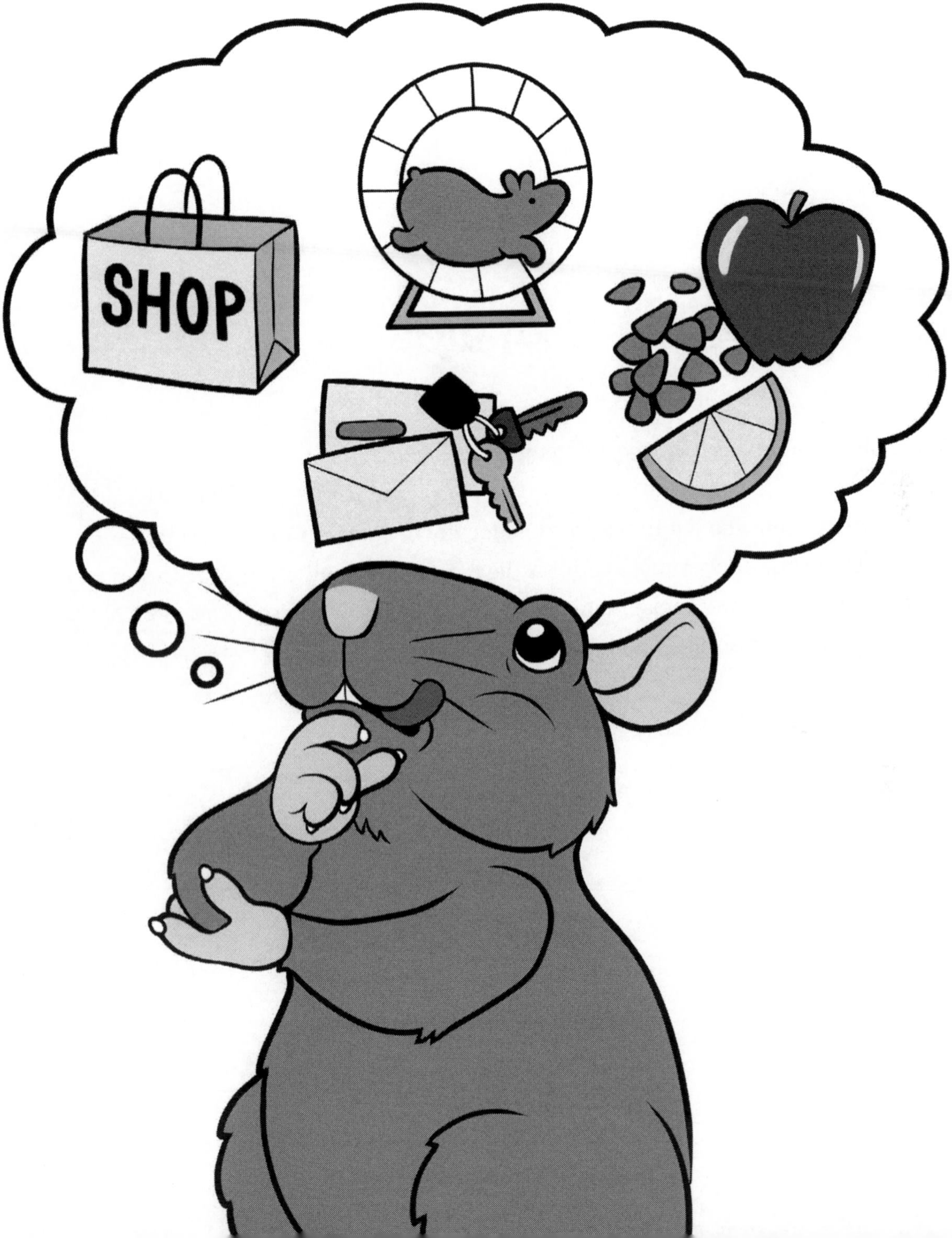
SHOP

24. Try Basket Weaving

Okay, maybe not *basket weaving*, but a menial, repetitive task. When you perform an undemanding task that requires no thought, your mind is free to explore other ideas. I know one person who habitually folds paper, my daughters knit and write, and I like to doodle. The less effort a task requires, the more your mind can wander and find open passageways to a grander imagination. Haven't you ever wondered why some of your greatest revelations occurred in the shower?

You can tell this to a hamster, but it probably won't know how to whittle or tie flies. It will eat, run in its wheel, and sleep.

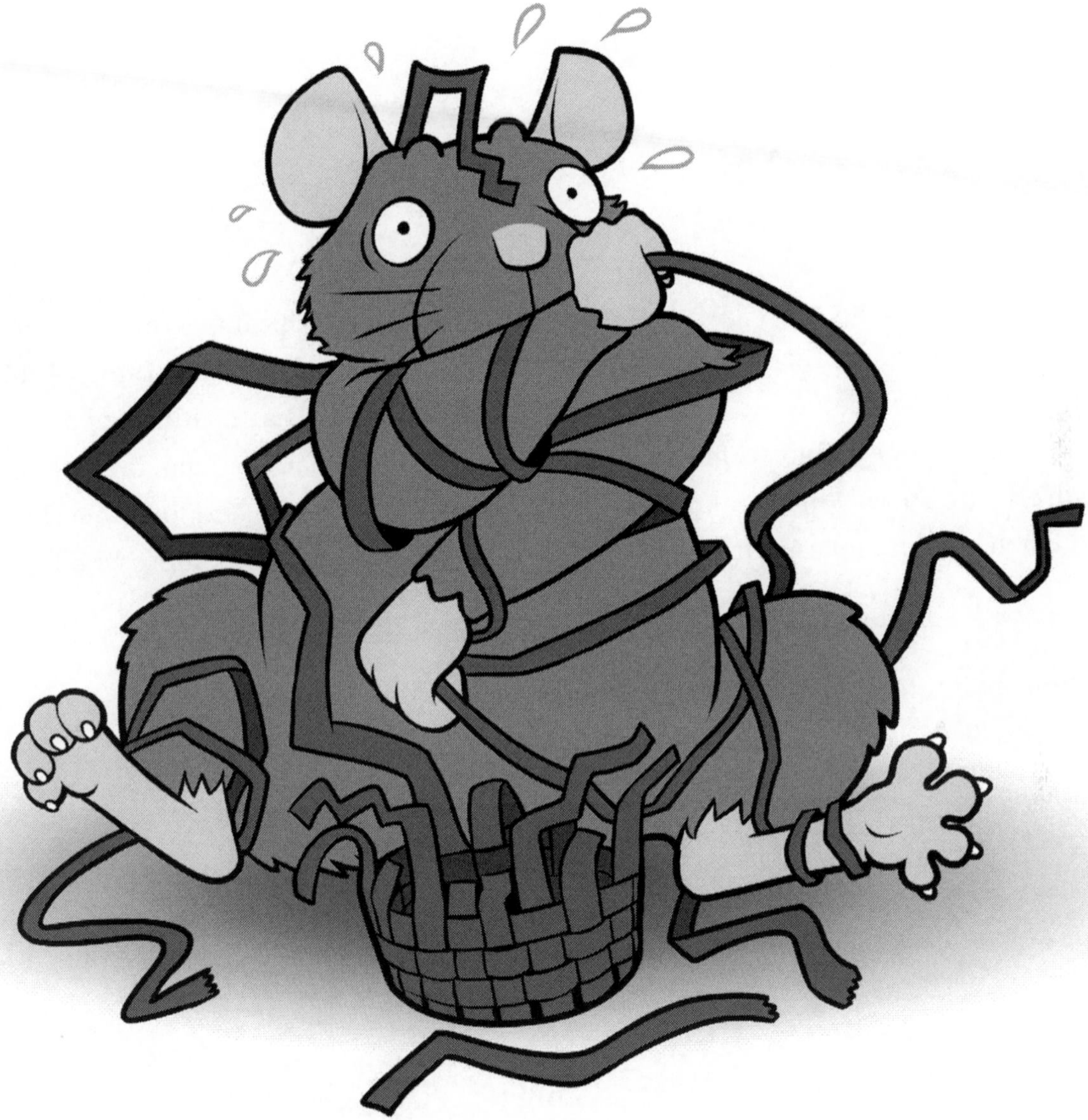

25. Daydream

Let your mind wander. Don't be afraid of occasionally losing focus. Enjoy those moments when you become distracted and you begin thinking of ridiculously silly things. While imagining yourself being successful in the future is a positive and exciting use of daydreaming, your imagination will also benefit from non-goal-oriented daydreams. Daydreaming opens your mind to possibilities that concentration and focus overlooks. And when you lose focus, remember to come back to what you were doing when your mind wandered.

You can tell this to a hamster, but no matter how much you stress it, the only thing the hamster will do is eat, run in its wheel, and sleep.

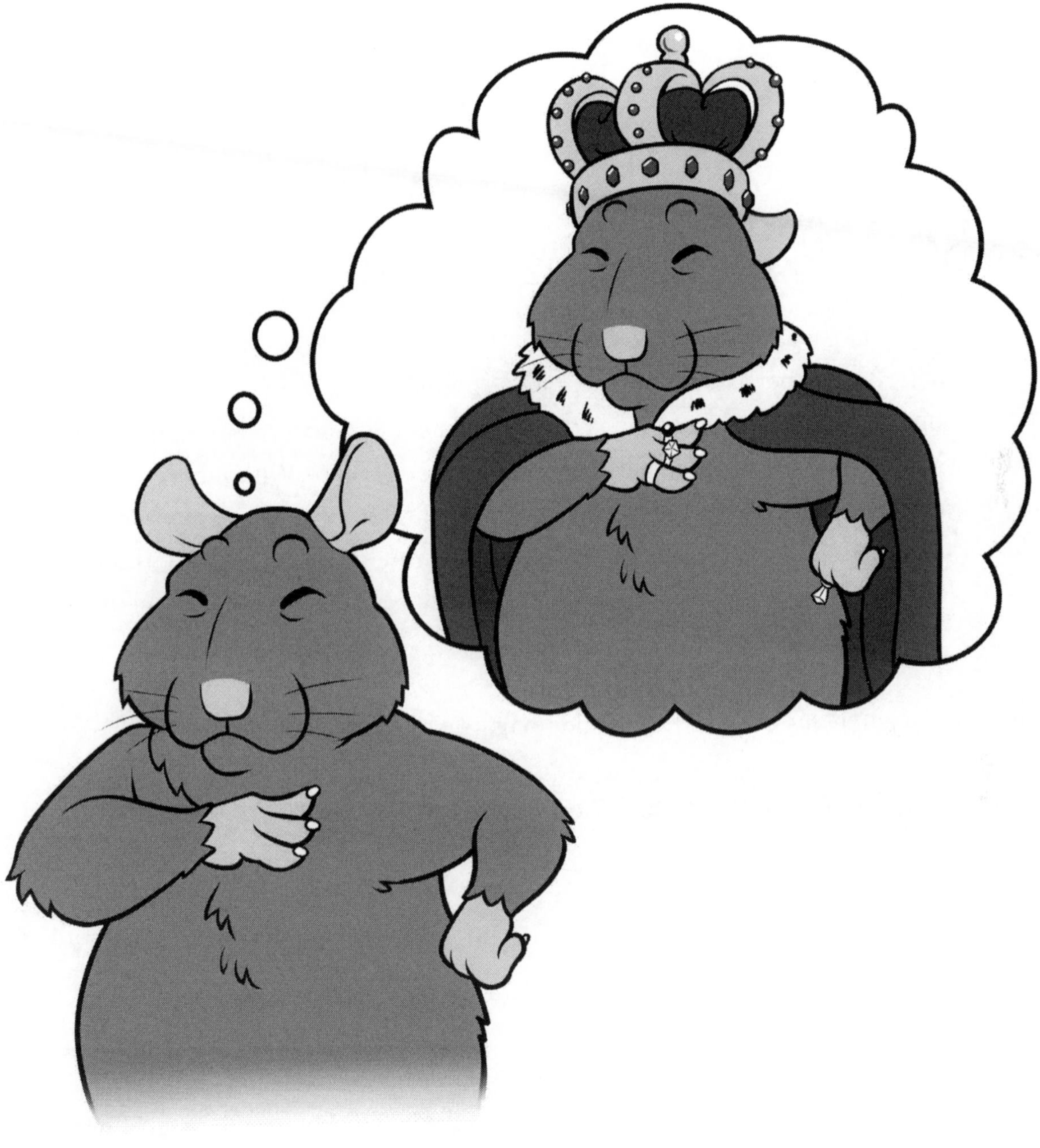

26. Be Elastic

Everyone fails. But the persistent and courageous bounce back. Some ideas may not produce remarkable results, but any idea you can imagine is worth chasing. Don't worry 'if it doesn't work out. You learn something new with each failure. Without mistakes, nothing would get accomplished. We would do the same safe task repeatedly, and we would produce the same results. Imagination requires you to be resilient and to continue creating and imagining even through the worst moments. Success awaits you on the other side.

Bounce back from failure, learn from it, and imagine a new plan of action.

You can tell this to a hamster, and it will listen and wiggle its nose. Then it will eat, run in its wheel, and sleep.

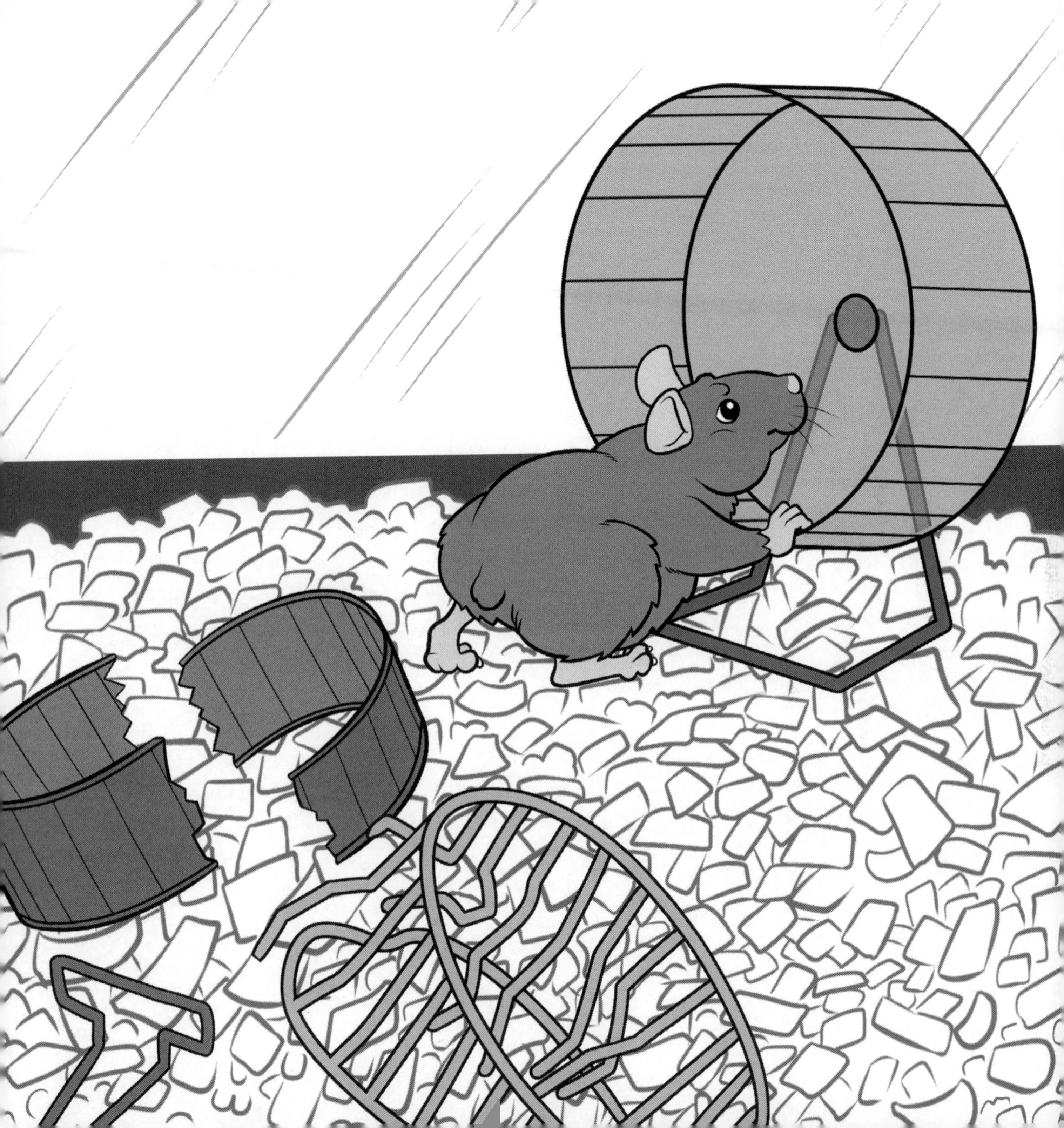

27. Build Brain Power

Put together jigsaw puzzles, solve difficult riddles or strategy games. By working on problems that have definitive solutions, your brain learns to solve problems by comparing options until it finds success. If you have ever taken a jigsaw puzzle piece and visually wandered around the puzzle trying to find where it belongs, your mind has imagined that puzzle piece in its proper place. During the search, your mind exercised its ability to visualize the solution. This effort to compare possibilities against each other exercises your imagination.

Your mind becomes more analytical when you do something challenging. Keep your mind growing.

You can tell this to a hamster, and you can give it the New York Times crossword puzzle with a solution dictionary, but it will eat, run in its wheel, and sleep.

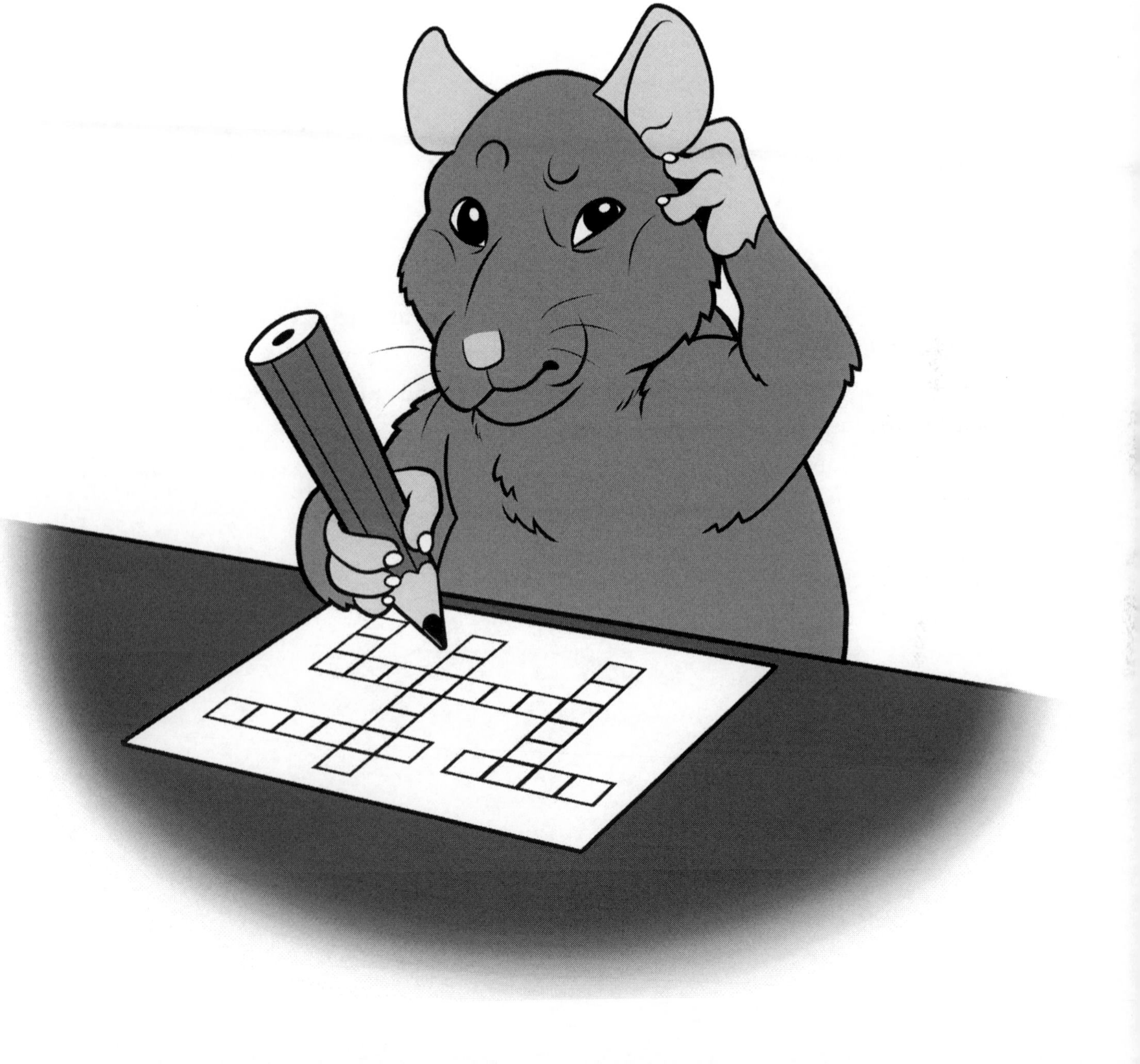

28. Stay Focused

No matter what you are doing, be present in the moment. There is a Zen teaching that says, *when you are washing the dishes, wash the dishes.* Whatever task you do, give it your entire focus. Do that task well. With increased focus and attention, you will learn to master that task. Your mental and physical memories will make it second nature so that it no longer requires the same intense concentration. As you master every task, your mind opens to receive innovative ideas and learn new ones.

You can tell this to a hamster, encourage it to do nothing but run on the wheel and focus on nothing, but... Never mind; a hamster already does this.

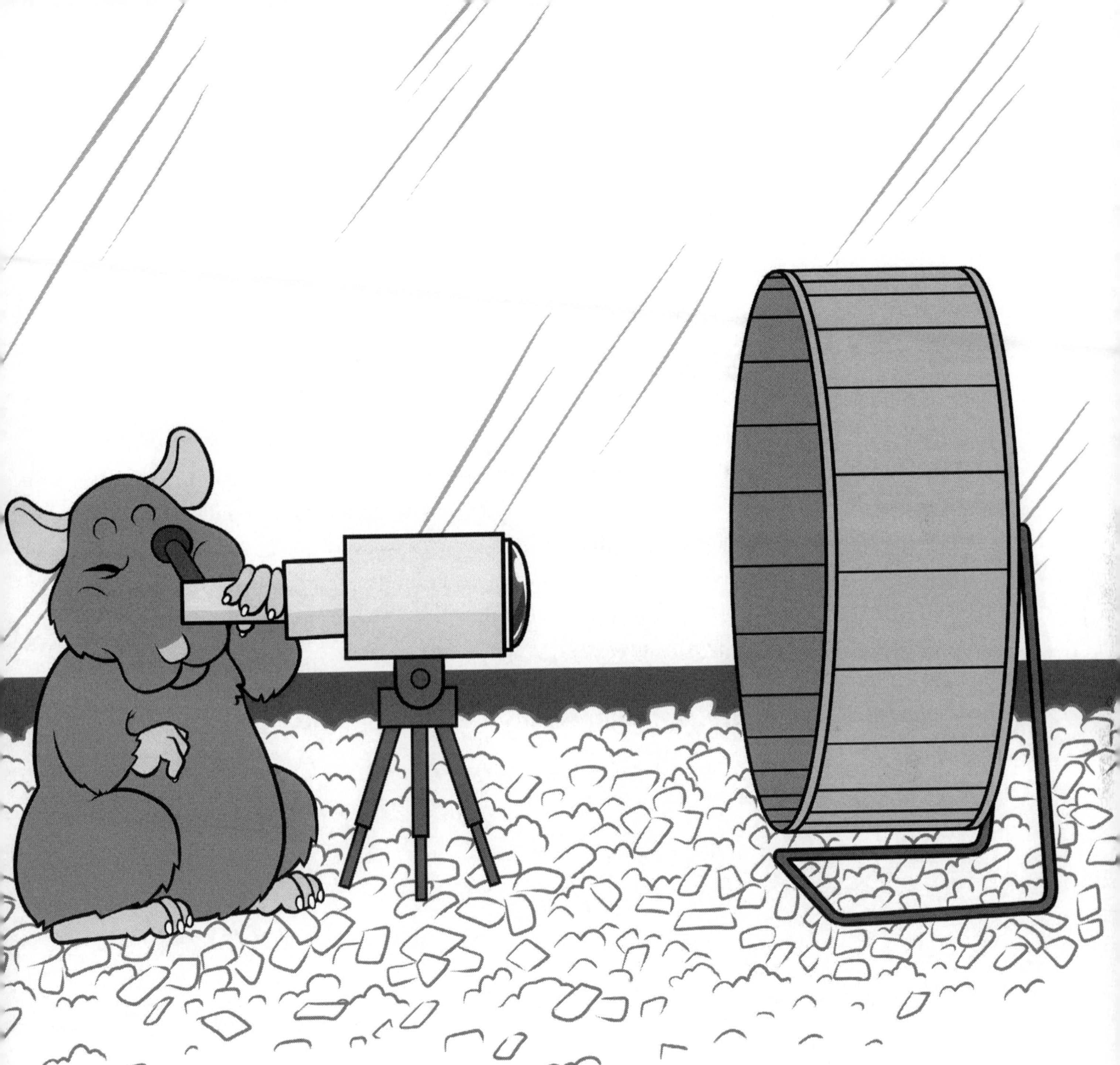

29. Get Physical

Your mind and body must live in harmony. The more you take care of your body, the more blood will flow to your brain. As your body exercises and works out, your mind becomes clearer, and much like performing menial tasks, ideas will surface when you least expect them to. Sitting at your desk and trying to imagine something new is nowhere near as productive as getting up and moving around. Get that blood flowing and grow your imagination. Create your own positive energy!

You can tell this to a hamster, put it on a treadmill ... Never mind; nothing changes.

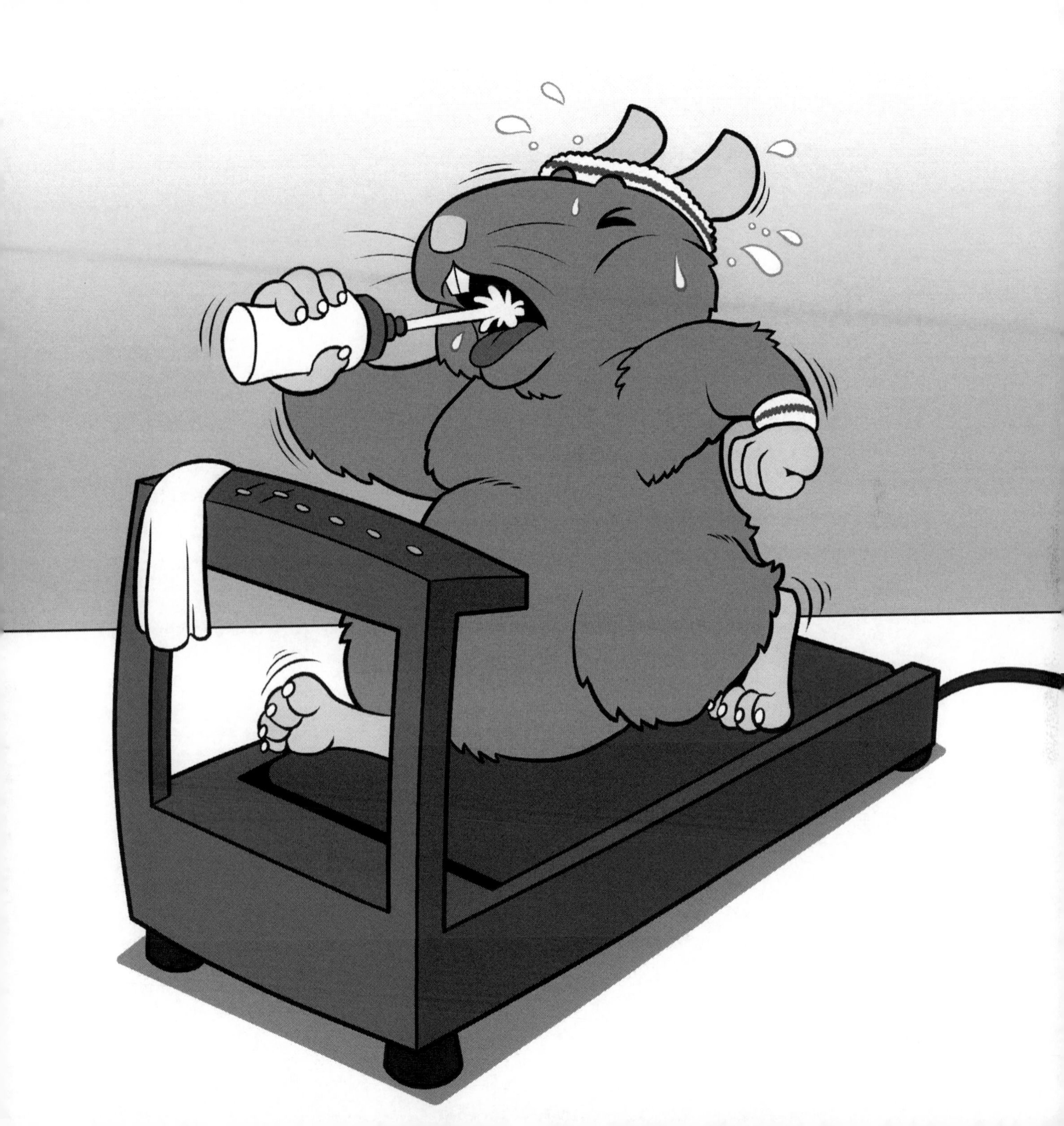

30. Believe in You

Trust yourself. Trust your ideas. Never second-guess them. While you may wish to second-guess the application of an idea, the idea itself is always good. The more ideas you generate without questioning their validity or value, the more crazy and novel ideas your mind will imagine. Embrace every idea that you have, because every idea is a child of your own creativity. It may not be a promising idea today, but tomorrow it could be the difference between success and failure. Treasure all of your ideas and believe you can be creative and imaginative. Always believe in the power of you. You are one of a kind. You cannot be replaced by a new hamster.

You can tell this to a hamster, but it will have no idea what you're talking about. It's a freakin' hamster! They are all alike.

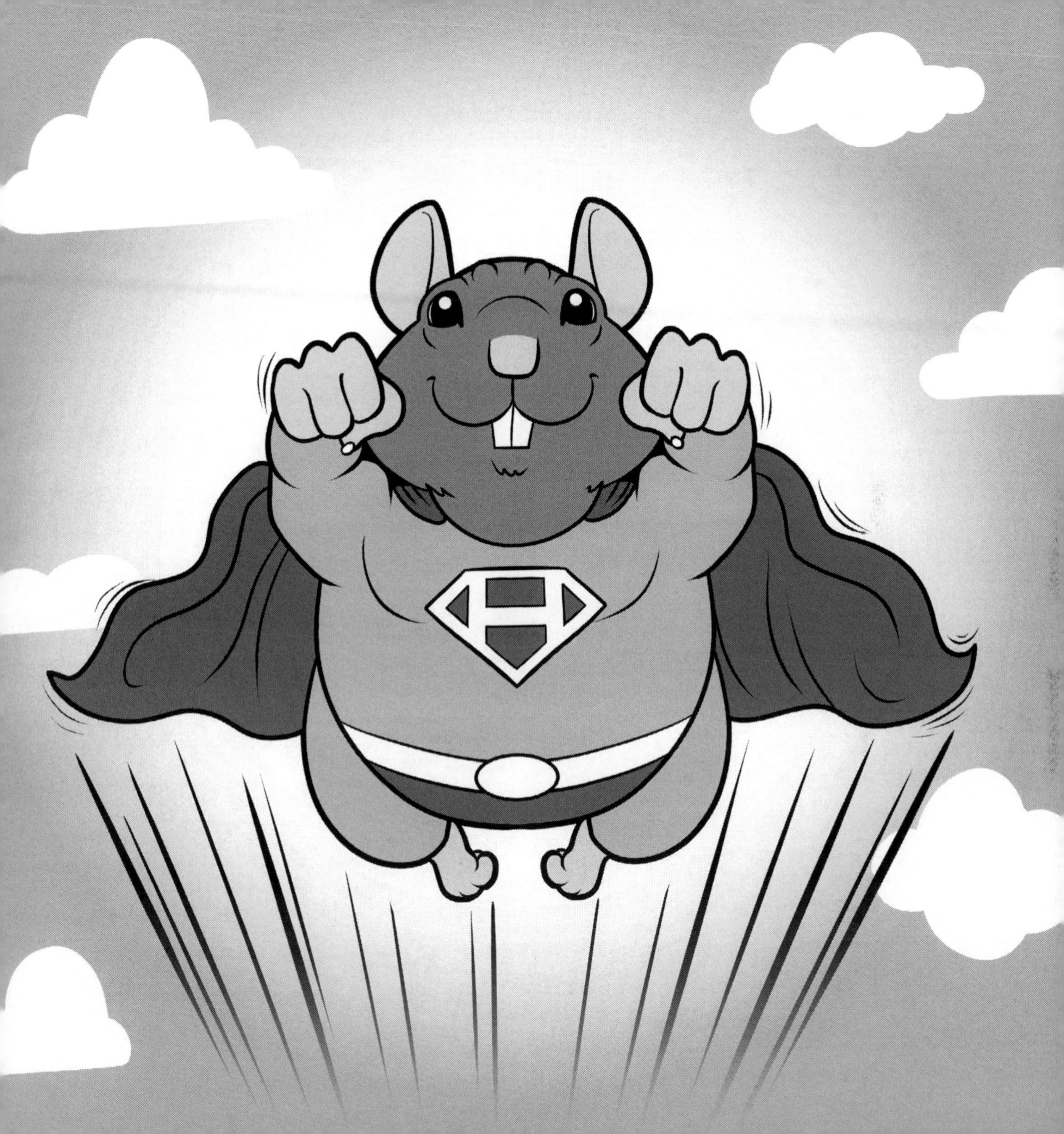

Don't be a hamster.

Get out of the
hamster wheel.

Imagine your future!

www.DontBeAHamster.com

ABOUT JOE CURCILLO

JOE CURCILLO is a consultant who helps company leaders engage their teams to enthusiastically achieve any outcome they desire. After practicing law for more than thirty years and managing his own successful law firm, Joe followed his passion for helping people communicate more effectively, and applies it to deliver speeches, training, and executive coaching that enable people to become empowering leaders.

Joe Curcillo earned his JD from Temple University School of Law. During his thirty-year-long legal career, he served as an adjunct professor of law teaching advocacy by developing a hands-on course that uses the art of storytelling as a communication tool. Joe now uses the skills of advocacy, storytelling, and management to guide his clients to be more effective. His work has been published in *Speaker Magazine, Sales & Service Excellence,* and *Pennsylvania Lawyer.*

Joe is also an internationally acclaimed award-winning mentalist entertainer. Using the powers of observation and the skills that he mastered selecting thousands of jurors, Joe "reads the minds" of his audience, stretching the power of perception beyond the imagination.

He resides in Harrisburg, Pennsylvania with his wife, the Honorable Judge Deborah Curcillo, and their daughters, Olivia and Kaela, who are both aspiring young professionals.

Don't be a Hamster!

These books by Joe Curcillo will get you off the wheel and on the path to greatness:

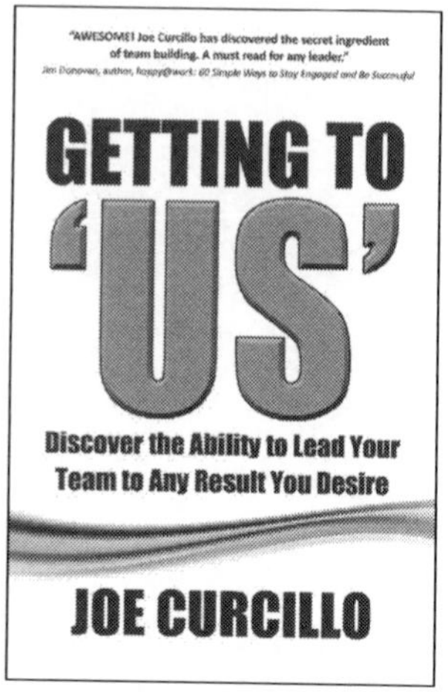
GETTING TO
'US'
Discover the Ability to Lead Your Team to Any Result You Desire
JOE CURCILLO

Getting to 'US': Discover the Ability to Lead Your Team to Any Result You Desire

Joe shows you how to take any group—even an apathetic or hostile one—and make it an enthusiastic, energized team ready to go "all in" for your cause.

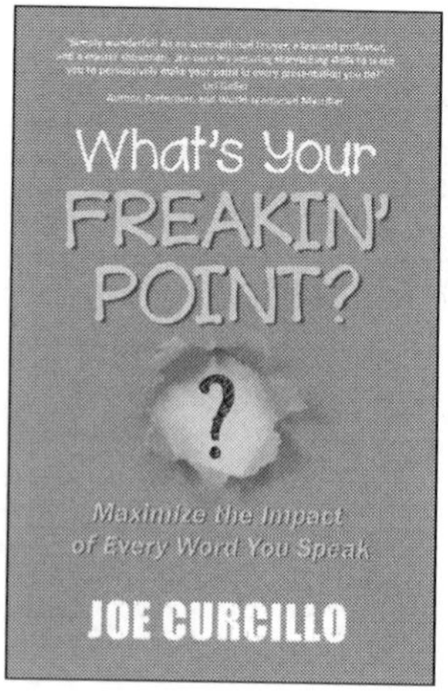
What's Your
FREAKIN'
POINT?
?
Maximize the Impact of Every Word You Speak
JOE CURCILLO

What's Your Freakin' Point? Maximize the Impact of Every Word You Speak

Joe shares his lifetime of experience as a courtroom lawyer and a professional entertainer to help you be an engaging, credible, and powerful presenter.

Order your copies today from www.TheMindShark.com

Want your next conference or event to be one for the ages? Book Joe Curcillo, America's premier mentalist/attorney!

Stage Show & Emcee: Think Loud! I am Listening.
A Mindreading Show Designed for Association & Corporate Entertainment

Your audience will witness and engage in the impossible. Above all, Joe provides the laughter and amazement that results in a memorable experience. With over forty years of experience in all types of venues, from Vegas casinos to New York corporate offices to cheap motels in Des Moines, Joe combines his former career as a "mind-reading" trial lawyer with his "charming sense of humor." (Well, that's what his mother calls it. Law school didn't take away his sense of humor!).

Keynote: If You Could Read Minds... Imagine...
A Keynote Full of Possibilities, Impossibilities, and MindShark Motivation!

When you listen, people will tell you what they are thinking... always. It's just like mind reading! The MindShark Motivation Experience is a dynamic message of empowerment and improvement. I offer a perfect balance of usable instruction and impossible amazement. In all ways, the aim is always to improve communication and persuasion skills. I predict that your people will learn to be better listeners, speakers, and influencers!

Breakout/Seminar: What's Your Freakin' Point?
Supercharge Your Communication Skills!

Skilled presenters and speakers understand the need to be on point. They know how to deliver a message that draws people in willingly. In *What's Your Freakin' Point: Maximize the Impact of Every Word You Speak*, Joe draws upon a lifetime as a courtroom lawyer and a professional entertainer to show your people how to be engaging, credible, and powerful presenters.

To learn more, visit www.TheMindShark.com, or email Joe at Joe@TheMindShark.com.

Notes, thoughts & ideas...

_____

_____

_____

_____

_____

_____

_____

_____

_____

_____

_____

_____

Notes, thoughts & ideas...

Notes, thoughts & ideas...

Notes, thoughts & ideas...

_____

_____

_____

_____

_____

_____

_____

_____

_____

_____

_____

_____

_____

Don't be a Hamster!
30 Ways to Spark the Imagination of Busy People
by Joe Curcillo
with Illustrations by Neil McMillin

Copyright © 2019 by Joe Curcillo

For information, contact:

THOUGHT EMPORIUM
LTD

Thought Emporium, Ltd.
3964 Lexington Street
Harrisburg, PA 17109
www.ThoughtEmporium.com

Book layout by Nick Zelinger

ISBN: 978-1-7324856-1-7

LCCN: 2018914448

First Edition

Printed in the United States of America

Made in the USA
Lexington, KY
05 January 2019